Growing up with God and Empire

CRITICAL LANGUAGE AND LITERACY STUDIES

Series Editors: Professor Alastair Pennycook, *University of Technology, Sydney, Australia* and Professor Brian Morgan, *Glendon College/York University, Toronto, Canada* and Professor Ryuko Kubota, *University of British Columbia, Vancouver, Canada*

Critical Language and Literacy Studies is an international series that encourages monographs directly addressing issues of power (its flows, inequities, distributions, trajectories) in a variety of language- and literacy-related realms. The aim with this series is twofold: (1) to cultivate scholarship that openly engages with social, political, and historical dimensions in language and literacy studies, and (2) to widen disciplinary horizons by encouraging new work on topics that have received little focus (see below for partial list of subject areas) and that use innovative theoretical frameworks.

All books in this series are externally peer-reviewed.

Full details of all the books in this series and of all our other publications can be found on http://www.multilingual-matters.com, or by writing to Multilingual Matters, St Nicholas House, 31–34 High Street, Bristol BS1 2AW, UK.

Other books in the series

Hybrid Identities and Adolescent Girls: Being 'Half' in Japan
Laurel D. Kamada
Decolonizing Literacy: Mexican Lives in the Era of Global Capitalism
Gregorio Hernandez-Zamora
Contending with Globalization in World Englishes
Mukul Saxena and Tope Omoniyi (eds)
ELT, Gender and International Development: Myths of Progress in a Neocolonial World
Roslyn Appleby
Examining Education, Media, and Dialogue under Occupation: The Case of Palestine and Israel
Ilham Nasser, Lawrence N. Berlin and Shelley Wong (eds)
The Struggle for Legitimacy: Indigenized Englishes in Settler Schools
Andrea Sterzuk
Style, Identity and Literacy: English in Singapore
Christopher Stroud and Lionel Wee
Language and Mobility: Unexpected Places
Alastair Pennycook
Talk, Text and Technology: Literacy and Social Practice in a Remote Indigenous Community
Inge Kral
Language Learning, Gender and Desire: Japanese Women on the Move
Kimie Takahashi
English and Development: Policy, Pedagogy and Globalization
Elizabeth J. Erling and Philip Seargeant (eds)
Ethnography, Superdiversity and Linguistic Landscapes: Chronicles of Complexity
Jan Blommaert
Power and Meaning Making in an EAP Classroom: Engaging with the Everyday
Christian W. Chun
Local Languaging, Literacy and Multilingualism in a West African Society
Kasper Juffermans
English Teaching and Evangelical Mission: The Case of Lighthouse School
Bill Johnston
Race and Ethnicity in English Language Teaching
Christopher Joseph Jenks
Language, Education and Neoliberalism: Critical Studies in Sociolinguistics
Mi-Cha Flubacher and Alfonso Del Percio (eds)
Scripts of Servitude - Language, Labor Migration and Transnational Domestic Work
Beatriz P. Lorente

CRITICAL LANGUAGE AND LITERACY STUDIES: 25

Growing up with God and Empire

A Postcolonial Analysis of 'Missionary Kid' Memoirs

Stephanie Vandrick

MULTILINGUAL MATTERS
Bristol • Blue Ridge Summit

To my beloved parents, Lois Lenore Vandrick and the late John Adler Vandrick, and my dear brothers Ken Vandrick, Ian Vandrick and Paul Vandrick, with whom I shared the missionary/missionary kid experience.

DOI https://doi.org/10.21832/VANDRI2326
Library of Congress Cataloging in Publication Data
A catalog record for this book is available from the Library of Congress.
Names: Vandrick, Stephanie, author.
Title: Growing up with God and Empire: A Postcolonial Analysis of 'Missionary Kid' Memoirs/Stephanie Vandrick.
Description: Bristol, UK; Blue Ridge Summit, PA: Multilingual Matters, [2019] | Series: Critical Language and Literacy Studies: 25 | Includes bibliographical references and index.
Identifiers: LCCN 2018032680| ISBN 9781788922326 (hbk : alk. paper) | ISBN 9781788922319 (pbk : alk. paper) | ISBN 9781788922333 (pdf) | ISBN 9781788922340 (epub) | ISBN 9781788922357 (kindle)
Subjects: LCSH: Children of missionaries—Biography—History and criticism. | Imperialism. | Postcolonialism.
Classification: LCC BV2094.5 .V36 2019 | DDC 266/.02373—dc23 LC record available at https://lccn.loc.gov/2018032680

British Library Cataloguing in Publication Data
A catalogue entry for this book is available from the British Library.

ISBN-13: 978-1-78892-232-6 (hbk)
ISBN-13: 978-1-78892-231-9 (pbk)

Multilingual Matters
UK: St Nicholas House, 31–34 High Street, Bristol BS1 2AW, UK.
USA: NBN, Blue Ridge Summit, PA, USA.

Website: www.multilingual-matters.com
Twitter: Multi_Ling_Mat
Facebook: https://www.facebook.com/multilingualmatters
Blog: www.channelviewpublications.wordpress.com

Copyright © 2019 Stephanie Vandrick.

All rights reserved. No part of this work may be reproduced in any form or by any means without permission in writing from the publisher.

The policy of Multilingual Matters/Channel View Publications is to use papers that are natural, renewable and recyclable products, made from wood grown in sustainable forests. In the manufacturing process of our books, and to further support our policy, preference is given to printers that have FSC and PEFC Chain of Custody certification. The FSC and/or PEFC logos will appear on those books where full certification has been granted to the printer concerned.

Typeset by Nova Techset Private Limited, Bengaluru and Chennai, India.
Printed and bound in the UK by the CPI Books Group Ltd.
Printed and bound in the US by Thomson-Shore, Inc.

Contents

Acknowledgements		vii
Series Editors' Preface		xi
1	Introduction	1
2	The Research	19
3	The Exotic	39
4	Treatment of Local People	51
5	Schooling	64
6	Learning Local Languages (or Not)	80
7	Gender	89
8	Race and Social Class	99
9	Implications	110
A Personal Epilogue		119
References		123
Index		134

Acknowledgements

Many, many people provided me with invaluable help, advice, ideas and encouragement while I was writing this book, and I am most grateful to all of them.

The University of San Francisco, where I teach, as well as its College of Arts and Sciences specifically, have provided great support for faculty research and writing through the years, including regular organized writing days and a dedicated writing room. I have benefited greatly from these, and I thank the university and college for their support. I also thank the university and the Faculty Association for their funding and administering the Faculty Development Fund, which has provided generous financial assistance for attending conferences and for other research expenses.

I also want to acknowledge and thank the people who set up and hosted a number of writing retreats at the Middlebury Institute of International Studies at Monterey library: Christine Pearson Casanave and the librarians, especially Kristen Cardoso. My attending those retreats was of great assistance in forwarding my work on this book.

Many individuals at the University of San Francisco have supported and encouraged me during my research and writing of this book, including, in particular, my colleagues, writing partners and friends Bernadette Barker-Plummer, Karen Bouwer and Kathryn Nasstrom, and I am most grateful to them.

Colleagues and friends from around the world in my disciplines of Applied Linguistics and English language education who have informed my work through their own work and through great conversations over the years include Roslyn Appleby, Dwight Atkinson, Diane Belcher, David Block, Suresh Canagarajah, Christian Chun, Deborah Crusan, Mary Jane Curry, Johnnie Johnson Hafernik, Adrian Holliday, Bill Johnston, Yasuko Kanno, Robert Kohls, Laura Kusaka, Ena Lee, Mario López-Gopar, Dorothy Messerschmitt, Brian Morgan, Bonny Norton, Hanako Okada, Brian Paltridge, Alastair Pennycook, Matthew Prior, Sue Starfield, Manka Varghese and Reiko Yoshihara. Special thanks go to Vaidehi Ramanathan for her invaluable feedback.

In a category of their own are the women in a group that has been very important to me in so many ways, the Sister Scholars. These are women from all over the US and the world who are teachers and scholars in Education and Applied Linguistics: Rachel Grant, Ryuko Kubota, Angel Lin, Suhanthie Motha, Gertrude Tinker Sachs and Shelley Wong. In this group, we not only present papers and publish together, but also provide each other with professional and personal support, encouragement, role models, information, inspiration, conversation, praise, consolation, shoring up, laughter and friendship. I feel extremely fortunate to be part of this group.

Very special and heartfelt thanks go to three great colleagues in my field(s), each an amazing scholar, role model and staunch friend, each of whom has always been there for me, and with each of whom I have had many wonderful, rich, deep conversations over the years: Sarah Benesch, Suhanthie Motha and Christine Pearson Casanave. Sarah's pathbreaking work on critical pedagogy opened my eyes some 25 years ago and has influenced me and my work ever since; she introduced me to so many ideas and people, and she has always been a great inspiration and a close and generous friend. I deeply admire and always learn from Suhanthie and her brilliant work, as well as her passionate commitment to social justice, and I so appreciate and treasure her thoughtful, generous and unwavering support and friendship. And I can never give enough credit and thanks to my longtime colleague and dear friend, Christine. For decades, Chris and I have shared ideas, read each other's drafts, co-edited a book, created and shared writing retreats (formal and informal), kept up a constant stream of emails and encouraged each other in our work no matter what.

Thank you to Gary Barkhuizen, whose publishing of an early iteration of my then nascent research on 'missionary kid' memoirs as a chapter in his edited book *Narrative Research in Applied Linguistics* launched my writing of the book which you are now reading.

I feel very fortunate to be published by Multilingual Matters. The terrific people there are thoughtful, inspiring, supportive and flexible. Special thanks to my editor, Anna Roderick, who has been wonderful to work with. Many thanks too to the editors of the Critical Language and Literacy Studies series, of which this book is a part: Ryuko Kubota, Brian Morgan and Alastair Pennycook, scholars whose work I have always admired tremendously and each of whose pioneering work has influenced me deeply over the years. Their selecting this book for publication means so much to me.

I thank my colleague and friend Bernadette Pedagno, who was very helpful with proofreading and other editorial matters.

I am grateful to the authors of the 42 'missionary kid' ('MK') memoirs I studied for this book. The memoirs are candid, thoughtful and moving documents, and I applaud the authors for sharing their experiences and their feelings.

Finally, most important of all, I thank my family. I have been extraordinarily fortunate in my parents, Lois Lenore Vandrick and the late Dr John Adler Vandrick, the best parents I can possibly imagine: loving, caring, kind, brilliant, courageous, down-to-earth, open-minded, completely dedicated to making the world a better place and always there for their children. I am also deeply grateful for and to my three wonderful, kind, accomplished brothers: Ken, Ian and Paul, who shared the 'missionary kid' experience with me. They each have terrific families whom I love very much as well. I dearly love, thank and appreciate my husband Jahan, a great partner in life. I couldn't ask for a better daughter than my dear Mariam, and I thank her for all the joy she has brought me. She has brought two new family members into my life as well: her wonderful husband Pete and their beautiful baby boy, Emmett, greatly beloved and doted on by all the family. Being surrounded by such a loving family my whole life is the greatest gift imaginable, and has been the foundation for everything I have done.

Series Editors' Preface

In appraising Stephanie Vandrick's important new contribution to the Critical Language and Literacy Series (CLLS), readers are reminded of a longstanding tendency to view Christian missionary work in one-dimensional ways, either as the handmaiden of colonialism and the violent seizure of foreign territory, or conversely, as the manifest expression of Christian benevolence and service in lands where little opportunity has been perceived or acknowledged. Of the former, *The Bible and the Gun* (Davidson *et al.*, 1984) offers a compelling account of the collusion of religion and empire in Africa and the presumption of spiritual, racial and economic superiority that served to justify colonial oppression. Of the latter, a brief perusal of Christian missionary websites and their various denominational publications, provides ample celebratory accounts of this international activity. It is largely because of the depth of this divide, and the difficulties in talking across it, that attempts to promote dialogue between critical educators (critiquing the collusion of missionary work and English language teaching) and Christian educators (arguing for an understanding of spirituality and language education) have so often floundered (Wong & Canagarajah, 2009).

Vandrick's insightful book resists reductive polarities and foregrounds the many complexities of her topic and the experiences of those whose memoirs she has examined. These autobiographical accounts of missionary life provide a unique lens on the day-to-day workings of empire and the discursive infrastructure that underpinned colonial attitudes and practices (see e.g. Morris, 1968; Pennycook, 1998). But these accounts are also carefully examined to reveal personal contradictions, acts of resistance, and invaluable contributions to local development, education and health care motivated by a genuine affection for the people and communities in which missionary families worked. Of equal importance for this series are the ways in which Vandrick critically interrogates notions such as genuine affection or contributions to development while also extending the relevance of her study to current issues in applied linguistics and English Language Teaching (ELT) fields in which the professional and ethical parameters of evangelical Christian-run English language schools continue to be debated (Johnston, 2017; Wong & Canagarajah, 2009; Wong & Mahboob, 2018).

It is hard to imagine a scholar better positioned for such a project. In the field of TESOL and English for Academic Purposes (EAP), Vandrick is a highly respected researcher, well versed in postcolonial, feminist, anti-racist and class-based theories, all of which come to illuminate her analyses of the missionary memoirs. Her TESOL research has included important interventions in 'studying up', in investigating sites of privilege (Vandrick, 2009). As Thurlow and Jaworski (2017) note, to study sites of privilege is to study the production of inequality. Vandrick has also been a field leader in utilizing postcolonial, feminist, and anti-war literature in content-based EAP work (Morgan & Vandrick, 2009; Vandrick, 1997; Vandrick, 2014). She was also one of the earliest in the field to explore the scholarly value of narrative inquiry in TESOL and Language Teacher Education (e.g. Casanave & Vandrick, 2003) and continues to do so. These interests in literary genres and storytelling are not only professional specializations. They are also a personal passion for Vandrick, whose close attention to the craft of writing is shared in her popular online blog, Stephanie Vandrick Reads (http://stephanievandrickreads.blogspot.com).

Perhaps most significant, Vandrick's own life history serves as key motivation and point of reference in her study of missionary memoirs. Having grown up in India as a 'Mish Kid' (i.e. missionary kid), Vandrick's reflections on her Indian experiences both balance and enrich the impressive theoretical and writerly tools that she utilizes. Writing from the position of a child born to missionary parents, and analyzing narrative accounts by people of similar backgrounds, brings both a distancing effect (these are not the accounts of those that set out with missionary zeal but those inescapably brought into this sphere by birth) as well as a feeling of proximity (these are close, personal, painful, emotional stories of children born into particular circumstances). This is, of course, a difficult balance to maintain on many levels: the personal and the colonial, the religious and the secular, the familial and the political. Throughout the book, Vandrick clearly aligns missionary work with colonial power relations that seek to impose spiritual and cultural values on less powerful societies. It is impossible to understand the work of these missionaries, or others within the structures of Empire, without attending constantly to what Mignolo and Walsh (2018) term the *colonial matrix of power*. At the same time, she qualifies this critique by reflecting on the positive impact of her missionary parents in medicine and education, witnessed firsthand. In the course of writing this book, and in researching familial documents and discovering valued objects brought home from India – her father's Telugu grammar book and dictionary, for example – Vandrick reveals a complex, emotional ambivalence, in her own words, a mismatch between 'my negative view of colonialism and, on the other hand, my strong instinctive emotional attraction to some aspects of colonial days, especially in India, where I grew up.' Among the 'guilty pleasures' she divulges are novels and movies about the Raj as well as a nostalgia for afternoon English high teas further heightened with the presence of Indian words on tea menus.

How should we understand such guilty pleasures (i.e. desires, cf. Motha & Lin, 2014) in a book series devoted to the critical study of language and literacies? Is the emotional ambivalence Vandrick explores merely incidental to critical work? Or, alternatively, is it far more fundamental to textual repertoires attuned to broader forms of meaning making (i.e. embodied, ethical, eco-semiotic) and their worldly effects and affects? Vandrick is alert to such questions, expressing 'mixed feelings' around academic conventions and her evidence-based 'dissection' of the memoirs, wondering as well about the feelings of the memoirists should they read her analyses. Clearly, for Vandrick, it is not sufficient to simply read the 'truth of the text' with a presumption/arrogance of rational objectivity, itself a residue of Eurocentric, colonial epistemologies. Arguably, Vandrick's transgressive strengths reside precisely in the productive hybridity she has forged from emotional, rational, aesthetic, and deeply introspective domains as well as critical reflexivity of her privilege. Vandrick's hybrid approach foregrounds consideration of not only *how* we read texts but also how we read the *reader* of texts in specific places and times. What particularities allows *this* reader to identify/create intertextualities or absences not recognized by others (see e.g. the relational, eco-semiotic notion of *affordances*, van Lier, 2004)? Vandrick's investigation does not therefore help us absolve ourselves from the injustices, collusions, denigrations and defamities of colonialism, but it helps us see both the complexities behind some of these relations and the complexities behind our reading and writing positionalities. If we want to engage in the ongoing project of *decoloniality* – a project as relevant today as it was in the middle of the 20th century (Mignolo & Walsh, 2018) – we need to avoid dealing only in simplistic accounts of colonial brutality (without ignoring them either).

In the context of this book series, a few points of comparison with two other books - Pennycook's (2012) *Language and Mobility: Unexpected Places*, and Bill Johnston's (2017) *English Teaching and Evangelical Mission: The Case of Lighthouse School* – are worth noting here. Johnston's (2017) detailed ethnographic study of evangelical Christians at

Lighthouse School in Poland, and his analysis of the unique, Bible-based curriculum and observations of its implementation and reception reveal both the pedagogical integrity of many language-learning activities, but also the proselytizing currents that often run through them. In several reading lessons observed on Daniel Defoe's *Robinson Crusoe*, for example, the book is reinterpreted as a spiritual redemption text, notably void of any reference to racism and colonialism in its textual underpinnings. This is one of several examples in which the Bible-based curricular strategy of 'digging deeper' around course content is selectively and narrowly applied at Lighthouse. Similar to Vandrick's study, Johnston's is a critical perspective that arises through careful ethnographic attention and site familiarity, as he carefully avoids doctrinal or idealistic proscriptions that are unlikely to further dialogue among critical, secular and evangelical language professionals.

Pennycook's familial connection to colonial India and his decision to work through these connections in a more personal and affective style, have several echoes here, as does his discussion of *mnemonic traces* (pp. 14–15). As with Vandrick's emotional encounter with her father's cherished Telugu grammar book, or the ritualized pleasures she identifies with English high tea, Pennycook speaks of a 'postcolonial sensorium,' the personalized semioses we attach to objects, whose immediate presence (touch, taste, smell) invokes memories of an absence (cf. Derrida's *trace*, in Pennycook, 2012) of distant times and places (see also Ramanathan, 2018). Again, these are exciting possibilities for critical literacies and language work. Both Vandrick and Pennycook, in this respect, extend our understanding of the rich, embodied resources that we bring to the production of meaning and of our understanding of texts – no longer static or bounded by page or screen. More recently, some of these ideas are emerging in work on sensorial and material literacies (Kell, 2015; Mills, 2016), entanglements (Toohey *et al.*, 2015) and assemblages (Pennycook, 2017, 2018).

Vandrick's critical analyses exemplify this new, hybrid orientation. Across these 42 memoirs of missionary life, profound absences are identified in the various stories presented by the memoirists. Conceptually organized around a variety of identity-based themes (race, class, gender, and their intersections), Vandrick notes the lack of awareness of concepts of privilege, imposition or oppression, as well as an 'airbrushing' of the negative aspects of careers when acknowledged in the memoirs. Passages revealing racial and spiritual condescension and exotic othering are also predictably evident. Less anticipated, for many readers, are Vandrick's accounts of the mistreatment of missionary kids, the trauma of their abandonment and sometimes physical abuse in boarding schools. Also less anticipated would be Vandrick's discussion of the worldliness of missionary kids and their grown-up roles as multiculturalists in the transition to a postcolonial and global world order. Of note here, as well, is Vandrick's highlighting of the important role of missionary women as early feminists opposed to the patriarchal attitudes and practices prevalent in the missionary enterprise.

The topic of language teaching and learning is a prominent focal point, particularly in the later chapters of the book. Reflecting on her own childhood experiences of Indian languages, Vandrick's reading of the memoirs indicates a general devaluing of local languages with only marginal interest in learning them for missionary purposes. In large part, such attitudes reflect the fact that many missionaries, past and present, have come from English-dominant countries (e.g. the US, Great Britain, Canada) that are complacently and/or stubbornly monolingual, a fact not unrelated to a history of TESOL methods favouring monolingual instruction and maximum exposure in the target language. Regarding ELT, Vandrick's provocative metaphor/adjective, 'missionary-like,' can be usefully applied to address the transition from English under colonialism to the current, global hegemony of English as a lingua franca, its persistent racialized inequalities (see e.g. Jenks, 2017; Kubota & Lin, 2009; Motha, 2014) and its hierarchies of ownership and professional (il)legitimacy (i.e. the marginal status of so-called Non-Native English-Speaking Teachers). In terms of postcolonial transitions, Vandrick also raises ethical and professional concerns regarding the growing prevalence of ELT as a covert vehicle for evangelical proselytization, a critical issue explored in detail in Johnston (2017) and by numerous scholars in the ELT field (e.g. Edge, 2003; Pennycook & Coutand-Marin, 2003; Varghese & Johnston, 2007; Wong & Canagarajah, 2009). At stake are not only issues of professional qualifications and moral/ethical responsibilities but also of socio-political values that align with evangelicalism and that may reflect conservative, nation-state ideologies inimical to the needs and conditions of communities in the global periphery.

Growing up with God and Empire: A Postcolonial Analysis of 'Missionary Kid' Memoirs is a wonderful contribution to the Critical Language and Literacy Series. At one point in the book, Vandrick, citing Czarniawska, notes that it is the professional duty of a researcher to provide or produce a 'novel reading' of their data. As both 'insider' and 'outsider' to these missionary memoirs, Vandrick has exceeded her obligation with both compassion and critical insight.

Brian Morgan, Alastair Pennycook, Ryuko Kubota

References

Casanave, C. P. and Vandrick, S. (2003) Introduction: Issues in writing for publication. In C. P. Casanave and S. Vandrick (eds.) *Writing for Scholarly Publication: Behind the Scenes in Language Education* (pp. 1–13). Mahwah, NJ: Lawrence Erlbaum.

Davidson, B., Ralling, C., Percival, J., Mitchell Beazley Television, Monarda Arts (Firm), and Channel Four (Great Britain) (1984) *Africa: Episode five: The bible and the gun.*

Edge, J. (2003) Imperial troopers and servants of the lord: A vision of TESOL for the 21st century. *TESOL Quarterly* 37 (4), 701–709.

Jenks, C. J. (2017) *Race and Ethnicity in English Language Teaching: Korea in Focus.* Bristol: Multilingual Matters.

Johnston, B. (2017) *English Teaching and Evangelical Mission: The Case of Lighthouse School.* Bristol: Multilingual Matters.

Kell, C. (2015) "Making people happen": materiality and movement in meaning-making trajectories. *Social Semiotics* 25 (4), 423–445.

Kubota, R. and Lin, A. (eds) (2009) *Race, Culture, and Identities in Second Language Education* (pp. 271–285). New York: Routledge.

Mignolo, W. and Walsh, C. (2018) *On Decoloniality: Concepts, Analytics, Praxis.* Durham, NC: Duke University Press.

Mills, K. (2016) *Literacy Theories for the Digital Age: Social, Critical, Multimodal, Spatial, Material and Sensory Lenses.* Bristol: Multilingual Matters.

Morris, J. (1968) *Pax Britannica: The Climax of an Empire.* New York: Penguin Books.

Morgan, B. and Vandrick, S. (2009) Imagining a peace curriculum: What second language education brings to the table. *Peace & Change: A Journal of Peace Research* 34, 510–532.

Motha, S. (2014) *Race, Empire, and English Language Teaching: Creating Responsible and Ethical Anti-Racist practice.* New York: Teachers College Press.

Motha, S. and Lin, A. (2014) "Non-coercive rearrangements": Theorizing desire in TESOL. *TESOL Quarterly* 48, 331–359.

Pennycook, A. (1998) *English and the Discourses of Colonialism.* New York: Routledge.

Pennycook, A. (2012) *Language and Mobility: Unexpected Places.* Bristol: Multilingual Matters.

Pennycook, A. (2017) Translanguaging and semiotic assemblages. *International Journal of Multilingualism* 14 (3) 269–282.

Pennycook, A . (2018) *Posthumanist Applied Linguistics.* London: Routledge

Pennycook, A. and Coutand-Marin, S. (2003) Teaching English as a Missionary Language (TEML). *Discourse: Studies in the Cultural Politics of Education* 24 (3), 337–353.

Ramanathan, V. (2018) *Language, Memory and Remembering: Explorations in Historical Sociolinguistics.* New York: Taylor and Francis Group.

Thurlow, C. and Jaworski, A. (2017) The discursive production and maintenance of class privilege: Permeable geographies, slippery rhetorics. *Discourse and Society,* https://doi.org/10.1177/0957926517713778

Toohey, K., Dagenais, D., Fodor, A., Hof, L., Nuñez, O. and Singh, A. (2015) 'That sounds so cooool': Entanglements of children, digital tools, and literacy practices. *TESOL Quarterly* 49 (3), 461–485.

Vandrick, S. (1997) Diaspora literature: A mirror for ESL students. *College ESL* 7 (2), 53–67.

Vandrick, S. (2009) *Interrogating Privilege: Reflections of a Second Language Educator.* Ann Arbor: University of Michigan Press.

Vandrick, S. (2014) The role of social class in English language education. *Journal of Language, Identity, and Education* 13, 85–91.

Van Lier, L. (2004) *The Ecology and Semiotics of Language Learning: A Sociocultural perspective*. Dordrecht: Kluwer Academic Publishers.

Varghese, M. and Johnston, B. (2007) Evangelical Christians and English language teaching. *TESOL Quarterly* 41 (1), 5–31.

Wong, M.S. and Canagarajah, S. (eds) (2009) *Christian and Critical English Language Educators in Dialogue: Pedagogical and Ethical Dilemmas*. New York: Routledge.

Wong, M.S. and Mahboob, A. (eds) (2018) *Spirituality and English Language Teaching: Religious Explorations of Teacher Identity, Pedagogy and Context*. Bristol: Multilingual Matters.

1 Introduction

> My own presence in India was linked ... to the British Raj ... All of us were interlopers of a kind, and ... it was clear that missionaries were as responsible for the spread of empire as the men at arms.
> ('Missionary Kid' memoirist Stephen Alter, pp. 299–300)

Overview of the Book

A well-known and very negative portrayal of missionaries is Barbara Kingsolver's excellent novel *The Poisonwood Bible* (1998), with its tyrannical protagonist, a missionary in Africa. In fact, very frequently when it came up in conversation that I was working on this book about 'missionary kid' memoirs, people asked me, 'Oh, have you read *The Poisonwood Bible*?' Unfortunately, in my view, it has become the most widely known fictional portrayal of missionaries. I say 'unfortunately' because I understand the negative, colonial aspects of missionary work, but I also believe that missionaries did many good things; nothing about missionaries and missions is simple. My point in this book is not that missionary work is intrinsically good or bad; it has been a mixture of both, and opinions differ on the proportions of each. I argue that it was and is, during and after the colonial era, part of the colonial enterprise, with long-lasting colonial after-effects. I make this argument not through grand historical narratives, but through highlighting evidence in the everyday lives of missionary families and their activities and attitudes, as illustrated in the 'missionary kid' memoirs that are the data for this book. The memoirists' childhood perspectives, although filtered through their having written the memoirs as adults, render transparent their being enmeshed in colonial thinking and behavior.

Missionaries, and by extension their children, were involved in the spread of religion and of aid, and they and their work were (and are) part of the Western colonial enterprise around the world. The work of North American missionaries during the 20th century was an aftermath and continuation of the empires of the British and other European countries, and was an inseparable element of a new colonialism and spread of empire carried out through military, cultural, language, religious and other means by North Americans themselves as well. The reverberations of these historical and social forces have continued for a long time. This book is a content analysis of 42 memoirs written by the children of North American Protestant missionaries over the 20th century. I examine these memoirs through a postcolonial lens, identifying and discussing instances of colonial attitudes and behaviors, but also addressing issues of intentionality or lack thereof.

The colonial aspects of the North American missionary project, and their connections with broader colonial beliefs, biases and behaviors, can be observed in the sometimes somewhat naïve and artless memoirs of the (now adult) children of missionaries, generally known popularly and in the literature as 'missionary kids', also known as 'MKs'. The MKs' perspectives are revealing, sometimes in a way that the words of their parents do not overtly show. Alter (1998), speaking more explicitly than most of the memoirists about colonialism, says the following about his missionary grandparents: *Socially my grandparents lived quite separate lives from the colonial authorities, but their experience of India was very much a part of the British Raj* (p. 25). He also notes that, years later, when he himself was at Woodstock, a missionary school in India, *[m]uch of Woodstock's heritage reflected a combination of British and American traditions, the vestiges of a colonial past* (p. 24). Schoonmaker (2011), more bluntly, writes about his missionary father,

> Dad was understandably a child of colonialism, sharing the typical colonial view that Western (in this case the British metropole) rule of India was at least a benevolent and benign, if not even divine, favor justifiably conferred upon a spiritually and politically blind heathen rabble devoid of intrinsically superior Christian morality, ethics, justice, and law, and in desperate need of deliverance. (p. 49)

Schoonmaker, showing that he himself did not, at least at the time of publishing his memoir (2011), agree with his father, goes on to say that the *murderous wars, moral corruption, and economic rape ... bloodshed, intimidation, and greed* carried out by the British in India were somehow rationalized by his father as *necessary measures to bring order and justice to a hopelessly chaotic and culturally inferior country* (p. 49).

By employing the lens of postcolonial theory, I realize that I seem to be taking a certain (somewhat negative) stance regarding Christian missionary work and its colonial elements, and so I am to some extent, yet it is not an unmoderated, absolute stance. By taking this postcolonial-inflected viewpoint, I am not 'judging' or 'critiquing' all mission work, all missionaries or, especially, all or even any MKs. The missionaries did much good during the course of their missionary work, as well as their sometimes problematic actions. The MKs did not have a choice about their circumstances. The ways they portray their experiences in their memoirs are, for me, data about the colonial influences that the MKs consciously or (mostly) unconsciously illustrate, as well as about the historical context. Although I am an MK myself, and this background has of course influenced me, I mainly write from the viewpoint of an early 21st-century academic, and do not believe that I should uncritically rush to judge or criticize people, especially people who were children at the time, without examining the historical and other contexts. I have attempted to avoid framing the illustrative excerpts from the memoirs as 'gotcha' moments in which I pounce on evidence of colonial attitudes in a judgmental way; instead, I simply attempt to somewhat untangle the connected and interwoven themes of colonialism and the missionary enterprise.

It is also important to note that there were of course differences among the various Protestant missions during the 20th century (as well as before and after). There were and are theological differences, as well as differences in the goals and focuses of the work. For example, some missions more explicitly attempted to convert local people to Christianity, whereas others focused on medical and educational work, and hoped that local people would then respond with interest in the religion. In this vein, the important Hocking Report (Hocking and the Committee of Appraisal, 1932), commissioned and carried out by a prestigious ecumenical group of Protestant leaders, delivered the major and controversial message that (as summarized by Hollinger, 2017: 69) 'What really mattered about missions was not preaching, but educational and philanthropic activities'. I note here too that missions from various other (non-North American) countries wrestled with the same issues about the purposes of their missions. For example, according to Vallgårda (2015), the Danish Missionary Society began in 1864, and continued at least through the early 20th century, with a focus on children and education, rather than direct evangelism. Although this sounds progressive, and although the Danish missionaries did much good, their work came with an Othering and patronizing attitude.

For the reasons above, and others, it is hard to explore all of the differences in various Protestant denominations in North America, let alone those in Europe and elsewhere. Even among the several denominations represented by the families of the memoirists studied here, there is not enough specific or systematic evidence in the memoirs regarding these denominational differences for me to carefully separate them out in this context. Thus, regarding this issue and others, I use the general terms 'missionary' and 'missionary kid', while fully acknowledging that this glosses over the diversity found among missions and missionaries.

I am also not arguing that the existence of Christianity in countries all over the world is wrong or inappropriate. The people in each country have agency, and now in most countries these local people are maintaining, shaping and expanding their churches and religious activities. Yes, Christianity in many cases arrived by way of missionary work, itself part of colonialism, and I critique those movements, but I do not here critique past or current Christian establishments and activities worldwide; that is not the purview of this book.

The missionary experiences of the memoirists in this study occur in a time period ranging from the early 20th century to the 1980s, with the bulk of them taking place between the 1930s and the 1970s. Some authors published their memoirs soon after their experiences, but most published them many years later, up to as recently as 2014. They lived in many different areas around the world, in Central and South America, Asia, the Middle East and Africa. The memoirs also range widely in the purposes for writing and the emphases of the books, as well as in the quality of the writing. A few are written by experienced academics or journalists, but most of the writers are amateurs. Motivations include writing to remember, to share experiences with children and grandchildren, to witness for religions, to provide a kind of self-administered therapy or simply to express themselves and share their experiences with wider audiences.

I believe that these memoirs, although sometimes artless (or perhaps because they are artless) provide useful documentation of a time and enterprise that is too little documented and discussed. The stories in the memoirs are necessary ones, and they add to our understanding of colonial and missionary experiences and ideologies of the 20th century.

I also want to make it clear that, although I am employing a postcolonial lens and analysis of the missionary enterprise, I understand that this approach is only one possible one, and of course does not fully explain that enterprise. However, the postcolonial lens does illuminate many aspects of missionary work and of the experiences of the children of missionaries, and that is what I hope will be the contribution of this book.

My analysis is set in the context of scholarly and popular literature and general beliefs about missionary work, as well as in the larger context of scholarship on colonialism and coloniality (colonialism being the actual historical events and related attitudes, and coloniality being the continuing effects of colonialism), especially the literature of postcolonial studies.

It also draws on other bodies of knowledge and theory such as identity work, literary studies, education and religious studies. My own interrelated disciplines of Applied Linguistics, Second Language Education and Teaching English to Speakers of Other Languages (TESOL) also inform this research. I address connections among missionary work, colonialism and English language teaching (ELT); like the promotion of Western culture and religion promulgated by colonialism and missionary work, the promotion and spread of the English language worldwide has consequences for local languages and cultures.

Missionaries

Christian missionaries who go from England and North America to other countries to teach their religion are commonly portrayed in literature and other media as rigid, dogmatic, un-nuanced, insensitive and self-satisfied. This was dramatically and vividly evident in the novel *The Poisonwood Bible*, mentioned above. In some cases, such as that of the character Somerset Maugham portrays in his famous story 'Rain' (2005, originally published 1921; later made into an also famous film), missionaries are also depicted as hypocritical. The novel *Hawaii* (1959) portrays author James Michener's view of the excesses of the missionaries' blunderingly overriding the cultures and customs of the local people, although his portrait is not completely critical and is sometimes even sympathetic. Other authors, such as the 'missionary kid' in China and mega-bestselling and Nobel Prize-winning author of *The Good Earth* (1931) and other novels, Pearl Buck, are more measured in their portrayals of missionaries as generally good but often flawed people; Buck also blamed the mission boards and administrators for inadequate selection and education of missionaries (Hutchison, 1987). Some prominent writers, such as Nadine Gordimer (also a Nobel Prize winner), also strongly disagreed with negative portrayals of missionaries. Hollinger (2017: 6) summarizes Gordimer's views as follows: '"The facts disprove" the old tale of missionaries as the inevitable agents of empire … the church's gospel produced many anticolonial activists', and '[m]issionaries were prominent in that important 'minority of colonizers, mainly of the Left … who identified themselves with the position that colonialism was unjust, racist, and anti-human'.

The term 'missionaries' refers to people who go from one country to another to bring their religion to that other country, as well as to do good, as they are called upon to do by their beliefs. The 'receiving' countries, as some missions call them, are generally less advantaged than the 'sending' countries, also a term used by some missions. Some terms used over the years by a wider group of people (e.g. scholars, journalists, government officials) for making these distinctions among prosperous and less prosperous countries include First, Second and Third Worlds (with the First being mostly Western countries; the Second being Russia and former Soviet Union countries and their close allies; and the Third being poorer countries, mostly in Asia and Africa). Another set of terms has been 'developed' and 'developing' countries. A more recent pair of labels has been the Global North and the Global South, with the North being the more prosperous of the two. Although I occasionally use one or more of these sets of terms, I realize that each set is both useful and problematic. In this book, the focus is on North American missionaries who go to Asia, Africa and South America. Of course, the concepts of 'missions' and 'missionaries' are more complicated than the above definition indicates. Sometimes missions are to people within the same country. Sometimes missions include medical or educational or other work that is not strictly religious, although done under the auspices of church missions. The term 'missionaries' has sometimes come to mean any kind of proselytizers, such as those advancing an agenda regarding certain political or social views. However, in any case, especially for those who are not supporters, the word 'missionaries' has taken on a negative connotation for many; it is looked at as an example of the imposition of the cultures and religions of more powerful countries or groups on members of less powerful entities. Missions are associated by many with colonialism and imperialism, and the cultural insensitivity that often accompanies them, and are demonized for that association.

Some scholars and others, however, even those who are not religious themselves, or not particularly supportive of missionary work, acknowledge that many missionaries have done excellent work in difficult circumstances. Recent research by sociologist Robert Woodberry (2012), for example, found a strong statistical significance between British missionary presence in certain countries in the 19th century and the current existence of stable democracies. I believe that whether or not one agrees with the evangelical aspects of missionary work, it is essential to note and remember the truly dedicated missionaries who did important and very useful work in the areas of medicine, public health and education, among other fields. The mixed feelings and opinions that many people hold about missionaries have, according to Hutchison (1987: 2), been a reason why 'missionaries and their sponsors have on the whole remained shadowy figures in narrations of religious and general history'. Hutchison is blunt in providing his explanation: 'The reason for such neglect is plain enough: these overseas Americans and their best-known objectives have seemed more than a little embarrassing'. As a daughter of missionaries myself, I understand this mixture of pride and embarrassment about missionary work, especially in view of the way it is often portrayed. This ambivalence in attitudes toward missionaries, and reasons for the ambivalence, is further explored in Chapter 2.

'Missionary Kids'

Third culture kids

'Missionary kids' are a subset of a group called 'Third Culture Kids' (TCKs) (Useem, 1966, 1976). An alternative term sometimes used is 'global nomad', coined by McCaig (1992, 2002), but 'Third Culture Kid' has become the more commonly used identifier for this group. As the label is most commonly used, TCKs are (generally) Western (most often English-speaking) children who, because of their parents' work, have lived a substantial part of their lives in other countries and cultures than their 'home' countries, but eventually return to their 'home' or 'passport' countries (Gillies, 1998; Gregory, 2002; Pollock & Van Reken, 2009; Nette & Hayden, 2007). Other examples of TCKs are 'military brats' and the children of diplomats and of international businesspeople. Since TCKS often feel they don't completely belong in either culture, their perceived place in the world is a 'third culture'. This term resonates with aspects of Bhabha's 'third space' (1994) and Kramsch's 'third place' (1993).

MKs, like other TCKs, are migrants, travelers, border-crossers and border-dwellers. They alternate between insider and outsider statuses. They grow up in countries where they are outsiders, yet their privileged status as Westerners, generally white, and generally with more money and resources than most local people, gives them a kind of insider/superior status. However, they almost never truly fit in while in these countries, no matter how much they would like to, or imagine that they do. Ironically, when they return to their countries of origin, they often feel like outsiders there as well. Thus, being a TCK is an identity not only during the years the child lives away from her or his home country, but also for the rest of her or his life. TCKs are often drawn to each other wherever they meet, and feel a kind of instant connection, even kinship, no matter where they lived as children. They are also frequently drawn to people originally from various countries not their own (Pollock & Van Reken, 2009).

Third Culture Kids find comfort in having a label for their situations, as well as a sense of belonging in discovering a common identity with others in the same situation. They celebrate the good and exciting aspects of their lives, but they also struggle with the more difficult aspects of their somewhat unsettled and fractured lives. Bechtel states that 'MKs are the ones who pay the price for the missionary effort across the globe' (quoted in Phemister, 2009: 1). Or as memoirist Seaman (1997: 5) put it, *We learned early that 'home' was an ambiguous concept, and wherever we lived, some essential part of our lives was always someplace else. So we were always in two minds. We learned to be happy and sad at the same time.* The memoirists in this study make multiple statements about not being sure where home was, of feeling divided, of feeling they didn't belong anywhere. Harvey (2009: 50), for example, plaintively asks *Where was my land? Where was my homeland? I did not know*, and Seaman (1997: 132) says that, years later, he is *still a refugee in my own country*. Similarly, Schroth (2011: 15) writes that she is *becoming not quite Indian but no longer American*, and that *forever, we will be hybrids*. She adds that *I am just plain weary of being different* (p. 34). Many of these statements are heartrendingly painful. Yet many memoirists celebrate their TCK/MK statuses. Lloret (2004: 7), for example, says, *I would not have traded my life growing up there as an MK for anything in the world*. A few memoirists identify so strongly with the countries where their parents were missionaries that they identify themselves as 'from' there. Orr (2003: 68), for example, talks about *my country, Nigeria*. And Friesen (2003: 47) describes himself as *this white African*. This split (often within the same person's feelings and statements) between positive and negative aspects of their MK lives epitomizes to me the complexities of TCK and MK experiences.

It might be of interest to readers that famous TCKs include the former US President Barack Obama; politician and diplomat John Kerry; actors Colin Firth, Viggo Mortensen, Uma Thurman and Reese Witherspoon; musician Freddie Mercury; and basketball player Kobe Bryant. Famous MKs include the writers Pearl Buck, John Hersey and Thornton Wilder, as well as the renowned, longtime editor of *Time* magazine and other newspapers, Henry Luce.

Here I use the term 'Third Culture Kid' as it has been used in virtually all of the literature, but I want to note that there is a somewhat troubling issue with the usual use of the term in that it is almost always used to describe North Americans who spent large parts of their childhoods in non-Western countries. One might wonder why immigrants and refugees from other countries to the US and Canada are not labeled Third Culture Kids, and in this sense it is a term with a huge Western bias (Vandrick, 2011a). Certainly the non-Western and the Western young people moving to a new country are perceived and portrayed differently, at least in North

America. Despite descriptions of difficulties that TCKs endure, the main narrative assumes a kind of well-traveled, culturally aware, sophisticated, even worldly character among these North American TCKs; these are positive qualities that are not commonly used to describe immigrants arriving in the US or Canada. There are some populations that seem very like TCKs as they are described in the scholarly literature, such as the 'Japanese returnees betwixt two worlds' that Kanno (2003) writes about, but they are generally not labeled as such.

Psychological and social aspects

One of the saddest things for me, while doing this research, has been reading the stories of those of the MKs, writing much later in life, who are still deeply negatively affected by their MK experiences, and have had to deal with problems in their relationships with their families of origin, friends, spouses, children, jobs and their 'home cultures' in North America. Often no one really understood their unhappiness and even psychological (intertwined with sociological) issues, including the schools and colleges that they attended 'back home' in North America (Isch, 2015). I briefly address both psychological and social issues here, because the psychological problems were often consequences of societal situations. The main areas causing psychological difficulties to several (but not all) of the MKs in this study and elsewhere were related to belonging to two or more cultures but not really to any; being separated from their parents when they were away at boarding school, sometimes at a very young age; and having trouble reintegrating into their North American lives upon return from the mission field. In later life, some MKs have had extensive therapy. Some have benefited from talking with other MKs and finding the strength that is often brought about by sharing experiences within a community; there are TCK and MK conferences, websites and other forums that provide connections and support. Some seem to be trying to work out their childhood feelings through the very act of writing their memoirs.

Walters (2007), a counselor who has worked with many MKs after they returned to the US, writes of many MKs' problems during their times on the mission field and/or after they return to North America. Their symptoms include feelings of separation and loss, feelings of being different from their peers in the US, lack of self-worth, loneliness, depression, alienation, anger, abandonment and sadness. Some, from the moment they return to North America, have a strong dislike for the US and for their schools and their churches, and in general are very unhappy. There is often a lack of understanding between the MKs and their non-MK family members and friends. Some MKs, Walters says, even have suicidal thoughts, or attempt or actually commit suicide. Little (2015), too, writes of the problems MKs often have with transitions, and with 'continued struggle creating and maintaining lasting attachments well into adulthood' (p. iv).

Walters notes that these feelings can be long lasting. For example, she writes of a 70-year old MK, Cam, who still struggles with the consequences of his MK childhood. He especially mourns that neither his wife nor his children can understand him, and that because he spent so much time away from his parents at boarding school, he feels he never learned how to be a good father. Walters also worked with a group of octogenarian MKs, and found that they were still affected by their MK experiences and the difficulties they had when put into boarding school at an early age, or left behind during their teenage or college years in the US or Canada for their education. They felt that their parents were more dedicated to their missionary work than to their own children. All of this is exacerbated by the need (or perception of the need) for MKs to keep up a good front and to present a certain godly, good, decent image, both in the mission field and on furlough in the churches and communities back home in North America; they were often reminded that they were representatives of their religion.

An example among the memoirists who had trouble with the transition back to the US is Bascom (2006), who when he returned to the US in high school, got headaches, slammed things, lay under his bed and exhibited other signs of psychological distress. His parents even took him to a neurologist. Only after a period of time in which he started to feel the stability of living in one place, and of coming home after school every day to his parents and family, did he begin to feel better. When another memoirist, Cordell (2008), returned to the US for college, she found that re-entry *was harsher than we expected. I found it desperately hard to adjust to college* (p. 157). Harvey (2009: 63) writes of the pain of leaving places and friends over and over again:

> How many times can a child repeat the cycle of separation and departure from recently formed friends? When the inevitable goodbyes began, I had to withdraw into that dark place of isolation. Eventually I preferred not to get involved in order to spare myself the tearing and grief that comes with each separation.

She goes to say that *As time went on, I separated from my parents. I became resigned to my fate* (p. 63). Similarly, when Van Reken was left back in the US for high school while her parents returned to the mission field in Nigeria, she was overcome with pain and anger:

> As the time for my parents' return to Africa drew nearer, I began to withdraw from them again. My anger grew and then gave way to the familiar pain, so great there were no other emotions left under which to hide it. But when I tried to express that pain, I always bumped into the reasons for the pending separation, and that locked me up. It was God's will that my parents return to Africa, and how could I argue with God? (Van Reken, 1988: 34)

Another sad consequence of the constant separations not only from parents but also from other relatives is that many MKs grew up barely knowing their grandparents. As Seaman (1997: 36) puts it, *because I was an MK, I didn't have grandparents*. It is heartbreaking that, to him, it is as if he didn't even have grandparents at all.

In the latter part of the 20th century, and into the 21st century, mission boards, psychologists, educators and others started to recognize some of the difficulties of MKs' re-entries, and since then there has been research done, counseling offered and other attention given to the problems (e.g. Austin, 1983, 1986; Bell, 1996; Collier, 2008; Jordan, 1992).

I do want to point out that not all MKs suffered from these problems, or suffered to a great extent, or suffered for long. Every MK, I believe, was affected by her or his MK background, for better or for worse, but many if not most were and are able to adjust at least reasonably well eventually, and to celebrate the good aspects of their having lived in different countries during their childhoods.

Brief History of the Missionary Enterprise

To provide context for these memoirs and my analysis, I outline here a very brief history of the Christian missionary enterprise. The history begins with the Pentecost (described in the New Testament) of Christian missions and missionary work. The Pentecost was the time soon after Jesus's resurrection when the spirit descended on the apostles. As Bhakiaraj (2016: 53) puts it, '[t]he New Testament church that was born on the day of Pentecost … learned right from the beginning that the formation of this reality, called the church, was integrally tied to mission. The church implied mission.' Christianity began to spread to various places in the world, but had a particular presence in Europe and, later, in the US. A very early 'missionary' was the Apostle Thomas, who is said to have established a Christian presence in India 'during the earliest (ante-Nicene) centuries of the Christian era' (Frykenberg, 2003a: 34).

In more recent history, and continuing with using India as an example, German Evangelical missionaries began arriving in 1706 (Frykenberg, 2003a: 47). The missionaries who were perhaps most prominent include the British Protestant William Carey, who lived in the late 18th century and early 19th century and is often called the father of modern missions. He worked in India as a minister, educator, translator and reformer. Another famous missionary was the Scottish David Livingstone, a medical missionary in various countries in Africa during the mid-19th century.

Very early in US history, churches and individuals decided to try to spread Christianity abroad through mission work. In 1812, five young men ordained as Congregational missionaries went by ship to India. Two of those missionaries – Adoniram Judson and his wife Ann – settled in Burma. Gradually the US (and soon after, Canadian) missionary project expanded. Hutchison (1987: 1) states that

> The foreign mission enterprise in its heyday (about 1880 to 1930) was a massive affair, involving tens of thousands of Americans abroad ... It sent abroad, through most of its history, not only the largest contingents of Americans – dwarfing all other categories except that of short-term travelers – but the most highly educated.

By 1900, there were approximately 5000 American missionaries. Statistics about numbers of missionaries in the world now are difficult to find, and wildly inconsistent, perhaps because the numbers are counted different ways. Some only count Protestants; some count Catholics and Mormons. Some only count long-term missionaries, whereas others count anyone who went on a mission trip, even one as short as one week. Current estimates range from 40,000 to 127,000. The influence of North American and other missionaries has been profound; by the year 2000, as many as two-thirds of the world's Christians came from countries where Western missionaries worked a century earlier.

The concept that mission work is an integral part of Christianity is very common to this day, especially among evangelical Christians. Castro (1978: 87) states firmly that '[m]ission is the fundamental reality of our Christian life ... Our life in this world is life in mission. Life has a purpose only to the extent that it has a missionary dimension'. His view of mission work obviously encompasses more than the specific work of missionaries actually moving to other countries, but the strength of his statement is representative of the essential role that mission work still plays in Christianity today.

However, a few missiologists (those who study the nature of missionary work) and other theologians realized how closely tied the missionary movement was to colonialism, and how the end of colonialism affected the missionary movement. Nygaard (2016: 112) believes that '[t]he abolition of the colonial age proved that part of the modern Protestant mission movement did not fare well without the colonial system'.

Evolution of the Missionary Enterprise

This analysis of MK memoirs aims to shed light not only on the colonial enterprise in which missionary work was embedded, but also on how and why work by North American missionaries (with roots in work by British missionaries) has changed over the years and into the present. Although the memoirs in this study mostly relate experiences from the 1930s to the 1970s, with a few in time periods just before and after, I want to acknowledge some of the changes that have occurred nearer to the end of the 20th century and into the 21st century, including changes in the ways that missions and missionaries have been perceived.

Robert (2014: 3) briefly maps the mid-to-late 20th century tides of missionary work. She states that '[b]y 1970 the end of colonialism and the Vietnam War had created a widespread backlash against missions', with a 'collapse of support for Western missions'. However, she notes, after the end of the Cold War in 1989, there was a 'resurgence' of religion, as 'secularizing and colonial narratives loosened their grip' (p. 5). She asserts that by 2002 the consensus among scholars of missions was 'that Christianity was no longer captive to the colonial West and that local and global are inseparable in the making of Christianity as a world religion' (p. 6). She also points out, as do other scholars, that 'the missionary is being redefined in North America', because of the existence of so many short-term mission projects, 'in an age when globe-trotting amateurs vastly outnumber career missionaries' (p. 6).

Nowadays there is an effort among some missionaries not to focus on the concept of West vs East, or on one-way missions (developed countries to developing countries). Bhakiaraj (2016: 56) emphasizes this view as follows:

> The missionary church that is being spoken of here, one must be clear, does not only mean the church in the west. On the contrary, it refers to the church around the world ... We should not speak about 'sending churches' and 'receiving churches'. Mission happens wherever the church is; it is how the church exists. Indeed mission is from everywhere to everywhere.

There is also some reflective, sometimes self-critical, writing by missionaries, and by scholars of missiology, about missionary work in which the missionary project, or at least some aspects of it, is questioned. In general these publications do not condemn the missionary project, but offer criticisms of some aspects of the work, or cautions and conditions about the work. For example, Nehrbass (2016) worries about missionaries' being considered 'Ugly Americans', and through an interview study examines perceptions of missionaries. He first lists some fictional and film portrayals of missionaries, and finds that, in general, '[i]n film and fiction, missionaries are graded on their ability to embrace their host culture' (p. 144) and 'are most positively depicted when their social action defends the rights of the powerless' (p. 145). Nehrbass goes on to discuss a criticism of US missionaries that local people sometimes have: 'the use of their "special status" to operate above the law by persuading people to convert' (p. 156). He states further, 'If westerners are seen as above the law, missionaries take extra pains to follow the law' and that '[w]ell-trained missionaries challenge the perception that westerners are most comfortable in their wealthy enclaves' (p. 159). Interestingly, Nehrbass also outlines another strategy used by some missionaries who are aware of negative perceptions of them and of their work: they 'purposefully distance themselves from that name [missionaries]' (p. 159).

One important change in the missionary enterprise is that overt, extended mission work is no longer (or in some cases was never) allowed by the governments of many countries, such as China and most Middle Eastern and North African countries; the main way that such work is prevented or at least hindered in these countries is that missionaries from other (mainly Western) countries are not given visas. Countries such as India and Turkey have strict limitations on such visas. In many cases, the visa rules have become much more restrictive over the years. 'Today, more than seventy countries are ... restrictive ..., up from thirty-eight in 1978' (Hale, 2016: xii–xiii). My own father, a medical missionary in India during the early part of the second half of the 20th century, applied many years later to do volunteer medical work with a respected medical group in India for a month or two, but was denied a visa because he had been a missionary in the past. In some cases, Americans and others who have gone to these countries without identifying themselves as missionaries have been prosecuted, deported or even jailed, for evangelizing.

Additionally, much of the work of the churches and other institutions established by missionaries has now, appropriately and as planned, been taken over by local people, who currently administer and support most of the Christian churches, schools and hospitals initially set up by missionaries. Also, and this is a very large and important reason for changes in the missionary enterprise, as alluded to earlier, many mission and other religious organizations send missionaries for far shorter amounts of time than in the past, often a year or less and sometimes as short as a week or two, often focused on very particular projects. Many of these are not career missionaries at all, but volunteers, or as Robert (2014: 6) calls them, with a note of asperity, 'globe-trotting amateurs'. This is in contrast to the standard lengths of service in the mid-20th century of approximately five-year terms, with one-year furloughs between terms. Many missionaries of that era made their mission work their lifelong careers. My great uncle Arthur Matheson served as a missionary in India for 45 years, from 1920 to 1965, and took very few furloughs in Canada during that time. My parents served two five-year terms in India, ending their missionary work in order that we four children would not be left alone in Canada or the US during our later schooling, college years and beyond.

Another change that affects the missionary experience nowadays compared with the past, even as recent a past as the 1970s, is that it is now much easier and faster to travel long distances. In the time period up to and including the mid-20th century, going back and forth was a major project, usually undertaken every five or so years, and often taking weeks each way. My family, for example, traveled by ship in the 1950s and 1960s, never by airplane. Further, communication is much easier and less expensive than it was in the past, so missionaries and missionary kids can now keep in touch with family and friends around the world by email, text, Skype, FaceTime and other modes of modern technology. When I was a child in India, we communicated almost entirely by letter, both within India and internationally. I still have, deep in my storage boxes, a small stack of some of the wafer-thin blue and green aerograms we sent back and forth to family members and friends. A long-distance call to North America was so rare that I do not remember ever hearing or participating in one. Deaths in the family and other urgent matters were usually announced by telegram; I remember with great clarity the day a telegram arrived informing my mother of her father's unexpected death in Canada.

For all these reasons, the traditional mid-20th century North American Christian missionary project, the one depicted in the memoirs studied here, with missionary careers being long-term, sometimes lifelong commitments, is becoming far less common, a part of history. Evangelical missionary work continues, but has changed shape in many ways in response to changing world conditions.

My Purposes in Writing This Book

I have several purposes in writing this book. One purpose arises from my belief that it is important that the 20th century missionary project be studied and documented, before the people and documents involved are no longer available to provide information and insights about it. In particular, although missionary work has been studied both by missionaries themselves and scholars of mission work, the specific topic of 'missionary kids' is very little studied in academic (or any other) literature; exceptions include Bellenoit (2007) and Useem (1976). Johnston (2003) argues that missionary writings contribute to the field and concepts of postcolonial studies. I believe that memoirs of MKs, the children of missionaries, also add unique historical and social perspectives, including the connections between the missionary enterprise and the larger colonial enterprise. Thus I hope that the memoirs, as well as this current research about them, constitute a small but useful contribution to the larger historical narrative of the 20th century.

A second purpose I have for this book is to shed some light on various types of privilege in the colonial context as found in the missionary enterprise. This privilege is (mostly inadvertently) illustrated in the memoirs through depicting the missionary families' surroundings, activities, attitudes, treatment of local people and exoticization of the countries where they lived, among other ways. I also examine gender, race and social class privilege in missionary settings.

In addition, the research provides connections with and context for the academic literature on sociopolitical issues in several disciplines, including my own interconnected disciplines of Applied Linguistics and English language education. A prominent example of such an issue is the controversy regarding some Christians' using roles of English as a Foreign Language (EFL) instructors to gain entrance to certain countries and then surreptitiously act as missionaries there (Edge, 2003; Pennycook & Coutand-Marin, 2003). This topic is further discussed in Chapter 9.

Finally, this research has social justice-related implications for other Western missionary-like projects such as those of national and international government organizations, non-governmental organizations and international charities; for their employees and their children; and for the complex, often vexed relationships among the senders/bringers of such aid and those who receive it.

My Positionality

As a missionary kid myself, and as a progressive scholar who knows of the serious harm at least some parts of colonialism have done throughout history, I am conflicted in my viewpoint of the missionary enterprise (Vandrick, 1999a, 2009b, 2013). Although I believe that many missionaries did much good, for many years after returning to North America, I was (as alluded to earlier) somewhat embarrassed by being the child of missionaries, and didn't discuss it much. Exacerbating this embarrassment was the fact that, as I moved into late adolescence, I no longer considered myself Christian, and have not done so since. However, I am still interested in the topics of religion and spirituality, and I have been influenced by a variety of religions and spiritual traditions (Vandrick, 2018). In later years, I grew to appreciate that my MK identity was an important part of my life, and of a certain kind of history, and that it had influenced me, and other MKs, in ways that I wanted to acknowledge and, eventually, study and analyze.

I grew up as the daughter of Canadian missionaries in India. I was there for 10 years of my life, from ages 2 to 7 and from 10 to 15. However, it took many more years to get to the point of being able to analyze the topic, years as an academic in Applied Linguistics and ELT, and occasionally in the fields of literature and Women's Studies as well. A major focus of my research has been identity issues such as gender, race and social class. My research interests include attention to postcolonial studies, as well as to narrative forms of research. In both my personal and academic lives, I have had a longtime passionate interest in literature, including memoir. These various elements of my life and scholarship started to coalesce into an interest in how my background as an MK and my career in academe inform each other, and I started writing about the connections. I gradually began moving beyond my own MK experiences and started accumulating memoirs of other MKs, leading to the beginnings of the current project, which in turn led to conference papers, a book chapter, and then this book. In this book, I explore both the experiences of missionary kids, not much written about in scholarly venues, and the colonial themes that are evident in their memoirs.

Structure of the Book

After this introductory chapter, Chapter 2 addresses, first, the colonial context of missionary work, and, second, the research for this book. Chapters 3–8 focus on six themes that I discerned in the memoirs, as follows. Chapter 3 describes the memoirists' frequent exoticization of the locales, people, events and customs they encountered. Chapter 4 explores the writers' families' treatment of servants and other local people, and the sense of superiority often displayed in these interactions. Chapter 5 delves into reasons the children learned (or didn't learn) local languages, and their attitudes toward these languages. Chapter 6 describes the MKs' education, especially at boarding schools, and the complex situations and issues that arose regarding education. Chapter 7 addresses gendered aspects of the MKs' experiences, including those affecting their parents and local people as well as themselves. Chapter 8 outlines some racial and social class aspects that shaped MKs' experiences. The final chapter, Chapter 9, discusses implications of this research, especially regarding connections among missionary work and the spread of the English language and of American culture.

Notes

(1) This book builds and greatly expands on the following previous publications: (a) Vandrick, S. (1999) ESL and the colonial legacy: A teacher faces her 'missionary kid' past. In G. Haroian-Guerin (ed.) *The Personal Narrative: Writing Ourselves as Teachers and Scholars* (pp. 63–74). Portland, ME: Calendar Islands Publishers (reprinted 2002 in V. Zamel and R. Spack (eds) *Enriching ESL Pedagogy: Reading and Activities for Engagement, Reflection, and Inquiry* (pp. 411–422). Mahwah, NJ: Lawrence Erlbaum Associates); (b) Vandrick, S. (2013) 'The colonial legacy' and 'missionary kid' memoirs. In G. Barkhuizen (ed.) *Narrative Research in Applied Linguistics* (pp. 19–40). Cambridge: Cambridge University Press.
(2) Throughout this book, direct quotations from the 42 memoirs are in italics.

2 The Research

The Missionary Project in The Colonial Context, Through Postcolonial Eyes

As early as the 16th century, but especially in the late 18th century and onwards into the 20th century, when Western countries such as England, through their governments, their militaries and their economic and business interests, took over many non-Western countries (e.g. among many, India, Kenya and Malaya), they not only governed, but also brought and in some cases imposed their cultures and religions as well. Then, even after most colonized countries became independent, often in the mid-20th century, Christian missionary work continued and intensified, thus extending the colonial enterprise in some aspects. Throughout this, the political, economic, cultural and religious enterprises were intertwined and hard to separate. Some missionaries and missionary scholars were quite direct in stating their beliefs that missions brought not only religion but also progress and civilization to other countries. Headland (1912: 3), for example, wrote of 'the influence of missions as a factor in the civilization of the world', and added that 'outside of all religious considerations missions had justified themselves by their influence in the government, the education, the science, the health, the wealth, and the trade of the world' – a rather grand claim.

In this book, I argue (especially in Chapter 1) that the missionary enterprise was in substantial ways a part of the colonial enterprise, albeit mostly unintentionally. However, scholarship about missions proposes various views about this connection, some emphasizing and some minimizing the ways in which the two were interconnected. Here I want to acknowledge that this is not a simple or one-dimensional matter. I do believe that the memoirs I studied illustrate colonial viewpoints, overtly or covertly, but I do not want to take a dogmatic, all-or-nothing stance on the matter. Below I examine some of the arguments against, or questioning, the claim that missionaries were part of the colonial enterprise. In this book, I am essentially exploring the question that Vallgårda (2016: 866) starkly states as follows: 'Were Protestant Christian missionaries from the western world essentially "evangelists of empire"?'. My thesis is that the answer to this question is at least partially 'yes', and that the 42 memoirs I studied offer multiple examples in support of that 'yes', but I also understand and agree with some of the arguments against that unqualified 'yes'.

Complicating the study of the missionary enterprise, and its connections with the colonial enterprise, is the fact that historians of religion and missionaries, on the one hand, and historians of empire, on the other hand, for many years operated separately, as if there were no connection (Porter, 2004; McKay, 2007). Further complicating matters, more recently, scholars from India and Africa have focused on the local religious communities, and the role of missionaries has (perhaps understandably) been marginalized and regarded as almost irrelevant (Porter, 2004). McKay (2007: 548) agrees, stating that the neglect by historians and other scholars of the 'vast archives' of Christian missionaries, containing a 'vast body of knowledge', is 'eccentric' and 'unprofessional'. Yet another relevant factor, according to Porter (2004: 5), is that mission historians have been looked down upon by 'secular' historians, thus minimizing the value of their knowledge and contributions. Porter's own view is that historians should note and remember that 'Missionaries viewed their world first of all with the eye of faith' and that 'missions … saw themselves much of the time as "anti-imperialist" and their relationship with empire as deeply ambiguous at best' (Porter, 2004: 13). However, although this may have been their own view, Porter continues, missionaries were often identified by local people as 'conquerors and colonizers, damned by proximity to [colonial] … administrators' (p. 13).

Even the idea and label of 'colonialism' have been questioned by scholars such as Frykenberg (2003b: 7), who states that 'colonialism … is more of a rhetorical device than a precise, scientific tool. It is part of a technology for denigrating, shaming, and shunning'. He goes on to claim that in relation to Christianity, the term has been used to demonize 'evil and exploitation' (p. 7). He criticizes the fact that scholars 'have long casually conflated Christianity with colonialism' (p. 8), although he acknowledges that there are some grounds for such conflation. His critique of the conflation of Christianity with colonialism is that it 'presumes that mindless people in India meekly suffered a forced imposition' of the Christian religion (p. 9). Frykenberg states even more forcefully that 'the last but most important of all reasons not to conflate or confuse Christian missions with Western colonialism rests in the essential participation, power, and presence of India's own Christians … who did most of the work and accomplished most of the truly significant results' (Frykenberg, 2003a: 61).

In a similar vein, McKay (2007: 548) states that:

[d]espite the popular association of missionaries with colonialism, the Christian missionary presence in the European empires was by no means always a supporting structure of colonial rule. Missionaries had the power to contest imperial racial divides, indeed they were often the strongest voices against racist officials or legislation.

McKay (2007: 548) also points out that 'missionaries' should not be grouped together as if they were all the same. Rather they were 'a disparate collection of individuals'. He goes on to say, in a spirited defense of missionaries as well as a clear challenge to the idea that missionaries were just like colonials, that 'in sharp contrast to the majority of colonial officials, the missionaries were in day-to-day contact with a cross selection of peoples from the indigenous societies' (p. 549). Further, they 'lived and worked among some of the most neglected colonial subjects. They learned the languages of those peoples, studied their religion and culture, and often spent their entire adult life living amongst them' (p. 549). Hollinger (2017) agrees, listing missionaries' many accomplishments abroad, establishing schools, colleges and medical schools, promoting literacy, and translating books into indigenous languages. In addition, he states that 'African women were able to use Christianity – for all the patriarchal elements in its scriptures – as a tool for increasing their autonomy, especially in choosing their own spouses' (p. 6), and makes the further point that American missionaries were among the first multiculturalists, bringing the world to the US, stating that from the early 20th century to World War II, 'missionaries were the primary source of information for most Americans about the non-European world, especially Asia' (p. 8).

Because of their extensive experience, the world of academe, diplomacy and government started to value them and their expertise. 'World War II and the decolonization of Asia and Africa catapulted missionary-connected Americans into positions of unprecedented importance because they were so far ahead of the global curve' (Hollinger, 2017: 8). One fascinating and telling anecdote drives this point home: 'When Edwin Reischauer was installed as the head of a military language training program in 1942, he noticed, upon arriving in Washington to take charge of his unit, that every person in the room was, like him, a child of missionaries, or had spent time as a missionary' (Hollinger, 2017: 8–9). Hollinger also points out that it was the 'mainline' or 'ecumenical' denominations, rather than the more fundamentalist and evangelical ones, that were more socially connected, more liberal and emphasized the social justice aspects of missionary work, especially among the most prominent missionaries, who were often scholars and leaders as well. One example of missionary leadership toward multiculturalism and social justice given by Hollinger is that of the former missionary in China, Walter Judd, who became a Republican congressman who insisted on 'the strategic importance of Asia', was a leading advocate of legislation easing restrictions on immigration from China and fought for the statehood of Hawaii. Judd was especially well known for a very important civil rights achievement: 'his successful campaign to eliminate the barrier to naturalized citizenship for non-white immigrants' (Hollinger, 2017: 185). Judd exemplified Hollinger's thesis that missionaries and former missionaries were multiculturalists and advocates for people from various cultures and of various races. In the same vein, Hollinger points out that missionaries and former missionaries were very involved in such international work as the church-sponsored foreign aid organization International Voluntary Services, a precursor to the Peace Corps, and highlights the literacy work of ex-missionary Frank Laubach. In addition, missionary-connected people and groups such as Edmund Davidson Soper, an academic and advocate against racism, fought racial prejudice in the US and elsewhere.

Hollinger also illustrates his argument that missionaries, and MKs, contributed greatly to the multiculturalism of America through his examination of the category of 'mish kids' (another name for 'missionary kids'). He describes these children of missionaries as almost always feeling that they had been 'born a foreigner', and that they were 'strangers at home' (Hollinger, 2017: 15). He believes that they were 'more immersed in foreign cultures more deeply than most of the American children raised abroad' (such as those in business, military, or diplomatic families) (p. 16). They were also, as mentioned elsewhere, more likely to attend and graduate from college and to earn postgraduate degrees than other Americans, as well as being more 'cosmopolitan in their interests' (p. 16). One example he gives is that of graduates from Kodaikanal School in India in 1949 (the school that I myself attended some years later): 11 of the 12 male graduates (but note the gender issue here) that year later earned either MD or PhD degrees. Hollinger does acknowledge, though, the psychological stresses (discussed in Chapter 1 of this book) experienced by many missionary children, caused by separation from parents while attending boarding schools and by the sense of not really belonging to any one culture, as well as by the difficulties of re-entering American society upon their return to their home countries. Hollinger lists some of the problematic situations among MKs, such as those who became alcoholic or committed suicide in later life. However, for those MKs who survived and thrived, Hollinger argues that '[t]hey learned it was hard to be a "citizen of the world," but they put more effort into it than most of their contemporaries' and he considers them 'proto-multiculturalists' and 'proto-world-citizens' (Hollinger, 2017: 23).

So the topic of connections between the missionary project and the larger colonial project is a vexed and still contentious one. The two forces of colonialism and mission work, although closely related and mostly in league with each other, did have some divergences and disagreements. For example, Viswanathan (1995: 431) points out that the British Parliament, in the early 19th century, publicly 'demanded a guarantee that large-scale proselytizing would not be carried out in India', but at the same time, '[p]rivately, though, it needed little persuasion about the distinct advantages that would flow from missionary contact with the natives and their "many immoral and disgusting habits"' (pp. 431–432). Viswanathan goes on to point out that the British government and the British missionaries had very different ideas about the education of Indian children.

Despite such various perspectives and tensions, it is hard to completely deny that colonialism allowed and (mostly, with exceptions such as noted above) promoted the spread of the Christian religion. This support from colonial powers was obviously very useful to Christian missionaries, but also somewhat tainted the missionary enterprise with its interconnected cultural and other types of imposition. After all, every country had and has its own religions, cultures and traditions, and was not asking for outsiders to come and teach its people about the Christian religion, although in some cases motivation was provided by the fact that those who converted to Christianity would obtain other advantages from the colonial powers. As mentioned earlier, this presumptuous imposition is why the word 'missionary' had and has negative connotations for many, not only in the formerly colonized countries, but also for many in North America as well, especially for 'liberals', 'progressives' and academics. To avoid oversimplifying, I would like to note again that some scholarship, such as that by Porter and by Frykenberg, outlined above, provides a more complex portrayal of missionaries and their work, rather than focusing only on the colonial and negative aspects. For another example, Bellenoit (2007: 6) questions the 'underlying presumption' of critical scholarship in the area, whose position 'has been to conflate ... missionaries with wider imperial prerogatives ... These arguments ... deserve significant qualification'.

Johnston (2003: 2) usefully outlines issues and questions regarding missionary work in colonial contexts as follows (in her case referring to

British missionaries, but the same arguments are relevant in the case of North American missionaries):

Generally, people are critical of missionaries' actions, seeing them as culturally insensitive and destructive. Some still celebrate them as introducing 'civilized', 'modern' practices to indigenous cultures. Others see them as the benign side of imperialism, providing a kind of moral justification for British expansion, and rightly argue that in some places they stood between the excessive violence of colonial expansion and indigenous peoples.

Johnston unreservedly states her own view that (in the 19th century) 'Christian missionary activity was central to the work of European colonialism, providing British missionaries and their supporters with a sense of justice and moral authority ... missionary activity was frequently involved with the initial steps of imperial expansion' (Johnston, 2003: 3).

Circling back to the work of Danish scholar Vallgårda, with whose question I began this discussion, we find that she feels that neither 'pole' of this argument is completely adequate or true. One 'pole' is the belief that missionary work is clearly a part of the colonial enterprise; the other is that there is only a little overlap. One group looks at colonialism as military, political and economic domination; the other has 'a broader notion of colonialism as a cultural, epistemological and even psychological ... endeavor' (Vallgårda, 2016: 870). Vallgårda herself chooses to reframe the discussion by choosing neither pole, nor something in between. Instead, she believes that, although the paternalism of colonists was often a part of missionary attitudes as well, missionaries worked 'at the margins of colonial society' (p. 871), and because they had no formal power, 'had to rely on persuasion rather than force' (p. 874). Vallgårda also demonstrates that indigenous people, in this case Indians, had a larger amount of agency than is often indicated in scholarship; they sometimes used the missionaries and their own 'conversions' as leverage; sometimes mocked missionaries; and sometimes 'appropriated and reshaped messages for their own purposes' (p. 874).

There are clearly arguments on both sides (although this topic is too complex to have only two sides, as Vallgårda (2016), among others, points out (see above) regarding colonial aspects of Christian missions, and connections between colonialism and missions. It is important to hear from non-European, non-North American scholars as well on these issues. The Nigerian scholar and church leader Okon (2014) has gathered some of these arguments from various sources in regard to missionaries in Africa, and although he focuses on European missions, what he and his sources have to say is in many ways relevant to the case of North American missions in Africa and elsewhere. Okon (2014: 193) defines colonialism as 'the imposition of foreign rule by an external power, which culminates in the control and exploitation of the conquered people'. He goes on to say that 'Africa was colonized through colonial machinery ... colonialism aided missions in 19th century Africa', that 'missionaries, traders, and colonial administrators had a common interest in Africa' (Okon, 2014: 192) and that missionaries 'came into Africa along with colonial administrators and traders with the plan to introduce Christianity, commerce and civilization' (p. 198). Okon then quotes scholars on both sides of the question. Arguing for the close connection between colonialism and missionary work, he quotes Sanneh (1990: 88) as saying that mission was 'imperialism at prayer' and that 'mission came to acquire the unsavory odor of collusion with the colonial power'. Okon cites Rodney's (1972: 277) labeling of missionaries as 'agents of imperialism ... agents of colonialism', and his statement that '[t]he church's role was primarily to preserve the social relations of colonialism'. Also cited by Okon, Kalu takes a more nuanced position, stating that 'missionaries depended on the merchants for transportation, supplies, and protection but they were constantly embarrassed by the morals of the merchants and their brutal exploitation of African societies' (Kalu, 1980: 7). Kalu also believes that 'missionaries colluded with the colonial government when it suited their interests and yet would also at times unleash virulent attacks on' that government (Kalu, 1980: 183). These various stances summarized by Okon illustrate some of the complexities of responses to missionary work and the way it has been regarded in relationship to colonialism more broadly.

Because of the historical timeline, most of the literature, scholarly and otherwise, on the relationships between missionary work and colonialism is in the context of European (especially British) colonial and missionary enterprises. As North American missions started and grew, many countries where they served were becoming independent. Further, the US and Canada, although certainly engaging in colonial-like activities, had fewer overtly colonial conquests in the mode of the earlier European colonial settlements. So the connections of North American missionary work and colonialism were less immediate and less explicit, but the legacies of colonialism were still very deep. Thus, although there is less literature about North American missionary work as colonialism, compared with such literature about British and other European colonialism, the influences are clear, and it is the evidence of these influences that I focus on in this book, while keeping in mind the counter-arguments outlined in this chapter as well.

Despite various scholarly and non-scholarly writings on missionaries, and even on their connections to colonialism, there is much less attention paid to this connection than would seem to be warranted. This lack of scholarly attention to the role of missionaries in colonial history exists to the extent that those very few scholars who do focus on missionary topics feel marginalized within the field of 'mainstream imperial history' (Cox, 2002: 8). Cox points out that '[i]n the large body of scholarly writing on missionaries, every historian has had to grapple in one way or another with the presumption of marginality in the master narratives of mainstream imperial history'. He further states that

> the presumption of marginality is so deeply rooted in the prevailing master narrative of imperial history that it is still common to come upon major monographs in imperial history, on subjects where one would assume that missionaries might be important, only to find them marginalized or ignored altogether. (Cox, 2002: 9)

Furthermore, despite what one might expect, Cox argues that '[n]ot only nationalist history but also subaltern history, and postcolonial imperial history, often share with imperial history the presumption of marginality ... the focus remains on those judged central to imperialism, the imperial administrators, jurists, and engineers' (p. 9). Even the famed scholar of postcolonialism, Edward Said, and his intellectual followers seem to marginalize the role of missionaries, according to Cox.

> In the rhetoric of unmasking that characterizes the Saidian master narratives, missionaries are often regarded as hardly worth exposing ... Added to the presumption of marginality is the presumption of imperial complicity, but it is a complicity often assumed rather than analyzed, interpreted, or explained. (Cox, 2002: 10)

If even noted scholars did not consider missionary work worthy of much attention as part of colonialism and imperialism, it is not surprising that the MKs or even their parents were very seldom consciously aware of being part of the colonial enterprise, and did not consider themselves in that light. The memoirs I studied certainly show almost no evidence of awareness of the concepts of privilege, imposition and oppression. Only a very few memoirists showed some awareness when they describe reflecting on their MK years much later, especially as they were writing their memoirs. Even then, there are only brief passages about the topic. In one of these passages, Harvey (2009: 229) writes strongly: *Indian people have been evangelized and harassed by missionaries for hundreds of years through colonialism and the fundamentalist mindset.* In her memoir, Orr

(2003: 29) writes that she *was shielded from so much of what went on around me in the pumping dust that was Nigeria in those days*, and that *I realize now what a telling picture we made, arriving in Eka, the whole moving project a vignette about privilege: makeshift trucks and movers groaning with a load of china and fine glass and mahogany furniture* (Orr, 2003: 74). Similarly, Alter, writing of his time in India, says (as quoted in the epigraph of Chapter 1):

> *Reading about colonial history I began to realize how my own presence in India was linked, in a peripheral way, to the British Raj ... All of us were interlopers of a kind, and from what I read, it was clear that missionaries were as responsible for the spread of empire as the men at arms.* (Alter, 1998: 299–300)

In his memoir, Coleman (2003: 10) writes of how Ethiopia was in a singular position in Africa of not being colonized, and therefore in the relationship of the missionaries to the local people there was *no colonial cringe, no special obeisance due to erstwhile white governors*. Yet when the revolutionary government came into power (in 1974, when King Haile Selassie was deposed), everything changed in the way missionaries were viewed. Coleman (2003: 10) says that *not until the revolutionary government came to power were we designated as the enemy. Suddenly we became Imperialists who had come to exploit the poor. Our whiteness became political in a way it hadn't been before.*

However, although the MK memoirs very seldom directly address these issues, the ways that they write about the people and experiences in their lives are very revealing of colonial and imperialist attitudes. It is this writing, these perspectives, these revealing choices of anecdotes and the words used to describe their experiences, that I focus on in this book.

The Role of Narrative in this Research

Narrative in the form of stories has been with us since the dawn of human life, and has a unique appeal. In academe, there has been a 'narrative turn' for several decades, but especially since the 1970s (e.g. Goodson & Gill, 2011; Maynes *et al.*, 2008; Polkinghorne, 1988). Narrative research has become more common as qualitative research has become more accepted in academe (Czarniawska, 2004). Willard-Traub (2006: 424), for example, says that 'increasingly ... approaches to writing that incorporate autobiography and personal narrative are being used by scholars ... as methods of scholarly analysis and argumentation'. In the area of education, Connelly and Clandinin (1999: 2) state that 'narratives of experience, are both personal ... and social – reflecting the milieu, the contexts in which teachers live'. Although there is still some resistance to qualitative research in general and narrative inquiry in particular, such scholars as Burdell and Swadener (1999), Daiute and Lightfoot (2004) and Witherell and Noddings (1991) write of its value. In my own work with Christine Pearson Casanave, we have argued for the revelatory value of narrative in research as follows:

> Narratives allow for understanding and connection in ways that straight exposition does not. Truth in academic writing, particularly in the more scientific fields, has been characterized as objective, as written in the third person, as distanced from personal feelings and experiences ... [W]e contend ... that there is another kind of truth to be obtained from narratives, stories, and first-person viewpoints, which people use to construct their realities and interpret their experiences. (Casanave & Vandrick, 2003: 2)

Feminist scholars have been particularly supportive of narrative as scholarly inquiry. Sharkey, for example, states that narratives have 'epistemological and methodological value because it is through narrative that personal experience – a rich source of knowledge – can be shared and theorized' (Sharkey, 2004: 498). Relatedly, making the connection between narrative and reflection, Willard-Traub writes that the 'turn toward reflective writing across the disciplines attests to the influence of cultural studies, feminist studies, and epistemologies that insist on the local and the "everyday" not only as valid objects of inquiry, but also as valid sources of authority' (Willard-Traub, 2006: 425).

In this book, I am mainly concerned with narrative in the form of personal narrative, with its interrelated subcategories of autobiography, memoir and autoethnography. I have categorized the 42 MK books in my study as memoirs rather than as autobiographies, although in truth, a few of them could be considered autobiographies; the line between the two genres is a blurred one. Zinsser has suggested that the difference between the two is as follows:

> Unlike autobiography, which moves in a dutiful line from birth to fame, memoir narrows the lens, focusing on a time in the writer's life that was unusually vivid, such as childhood or adolescence, or that was framed by war or travel or public service or some other special circumstance. (Zinsser, 1998: 15)

Although a few of these books tell the entire life stories of their authors, with the MK element just one part of the books, and thus could be called autobiographies (e.g. Braaten, 2010; Littell, 1995), the vast majority of the books specifically focus on the MK experience, and thus qualify as memoirs. Even the autobiographies all devote at least some chapters to detailing authors' childhoods as MKs, and often discuss the influence that experience has had on the rest of their lives.

There are occasionally other genres employed in the course of the memoirs discussed in this book. For example, in a few of the memoirs (e.g. Schoonmaker, 2011), the relevant events and feelings are told in a series of vignettes. One memoirist (Van Reken, 1998), tells her story in the format of letters to her parents, written in adulthood but as if they had been written at the time of her MK childhood. Wiebe's (1990) memoir takes the form of a sort of scrapbook, with many heavily annotated photos accompanied by fairly sparse text. In any case, all of these volumes, whether for the whole book or a substantial portion of the book, do in fact, as Zinsser (1998: 15) points out, 'narrow the lens, focusing on a time in the writer's life that was unusually vivid, such as childhood or adolescence, or that was framed by ... some ... special circumstance'. In this case, the 'special circumstance' is their lives as MKs.

The term 'autoethnography', although obviously related to autobiography and memoir, refers to a scholarly analysis of the subjects/writers of the personal narratives, incorporated into or closely interwoven with the narratives themselves. Bell points out that narrative inquiry 'requires going beyond the use of narrative as rhetorical structure, that is, simply telling stories, to an analytic examination of the underlying insights and assumptions that the story illustrates' (Bell, 2002: 208). This kind of writing is often found in the work of academics who write with reflexivity about their own lives, including their teaching and research. They ground their narratives in the professional literature, including theory, and use their stories to reveal truths. Some of the most well-known scholars who have pioneered the use of autoethnography include communication scholar Carolyn Ellis (e.g. 2004), sociologist Laurel Richardson (e.g. 1997), literary scholar Jane Tompkins (e.g. 1996), and Applied Linguistics scholars Suresh Canagarajah (e.g. 2012) and Alastair Pennycook (e.g. 2012). My own prior book on privilege and academe is partially in the form of autoethnography (Vandrick, 2009b). In this current book, I blend the stories of the MK memoirists with scholarly analysis in the contexts of related literature and theory. My analysis is also informed by my own background as a missionary kid. Some scholars label autoethnography as 'scholarly personal narrative' (Nash, 2004: 4) and 'personal academic discourse' (Spigelman, 2004: 3), and I find these terms useful and descriptive. I have called this blend of personal and academic argument a 'hybrid genre' (Vandrick, 2009b: 14). In this book, I am not only analyzing the narratives of the memoirists, but I am interspersing stories of my own MK experiences, and my feelings about those experiences. So the genre I am employing here is 'hybrid' in the sense of blending traditional academic writing with personal narrative, not only of the stories of the memoirists but of my own stories as well.

I am also interested in the fragility of memory, and in ways in which, as Mishler (2006) reminds us, we are constantly reinterpreting our past experiences through the lens of passing time and our ensuing experiences. Some of the memoirs I study here were written many years after the experiences the authors describe. For example, the late well-known theologian Huston Smith wrote his memoir as he approached the age of 90, some 74 years after he left China (Smith, 2010). Helen Bagby Harrison was born in 1900 in Brazil and published her memoir in 1983. In these cases, in obvious and less obvious ways, one can see how time, and later experiences, have influenced the way the memoirists remember, shape and tell their stories. For one example, I have observed that in general the older memoirists, who are the furthest away from their actual MK experiences, tend to romanticize their experiences more than younger ones do, emphasizing the positive aspects and feelings and somewhat airbrushing the negative aspects. I find memoirist Wiebe's (1990) title, *Sepia Prints*, as evocative in this regard.

This current project is partially influenced by the fact that I am analyzing other people's personal narratives using elements of MK life that became evident in my own autoethnographic work (Vandrick, 1999a, 2009b, 2013). As part of my approach to the MK memoirs, I use my own life experiences to interrogate and shed light on the experiences of the MKs and the ways in which the memoirists express their feelings. We know now that no research can be completely 'objective', and in any case my position as a former MK makes it hard for me to be completely objective. However, I believe that my experiences bring a dimension of understanding and connection to the memoirs that is useful, especially as they are moderated by my experiences as a longtime scholar.

The Research

The data

I casually collected and read a few MK memoirs over the years, especially when I was writing my own chapter-length MK memoir/autoethnography about connections between my MK past and my career teaching English (Vandrick, 1999a). They were of interest to me both personally and academically. I gradually started to see them not just as individual works but also as a body of work that intrigued me. I realized that not just reading but also studying and analyzing them as part of my research appealed to me on many levels. Such a project would bring together my involvement in several areas: my own life history, my academic work with international students, postcolonial studies and theory, literary analysis and the genre of memoir, among other interests. I then decided to use 'missionary kid' memoirs as my data for a chapter in an edited book on narrative research in applied linguistics, and gathered more such memoirs, a total of 17 at the time I wrote that chapter (Vandrick, 2013). When I decided to expand my study to this book-length project, I continued searching for more memoirs, up to the current total of the 42 examined in this book. I have since acquired more MK memoirs (e.g. Dopirak, 2016; Heusinkveld, 2017; Meyers, 1995) that I either had not found before or that were published after I had completed the analysis of the 42 memoirs, and therefore could not use for this study. I also know of a handful of novels (e.g. Johnson, 2009; Palmer, 2002) that are semi-autobiographical MK stories. I speculate that, even though there are fewer long-term missionaries now, and one would guess that there would consequently be fewer memoirs published, there are still many adult MKs out there (as many as 300,000 in the US as of the 1990s, according to Addleton, 2000; again, it is extremely difficult to find accurate and current statistics on MKs) who might still produce memoirs.

My criteria for choosing the memoirs were as follows. First, the authors had to be from the US or Canada and be writing about their own experiences as MKs in countries outside of their home countries for at least several years. (There is one exception – that of Kuegler (2005), who was from Germany, and therefore a slight outlier, but her memoir, story and attitudes are so congruent with those of the other memoirists that I decided to keep her memoir in the study.) I limit my analysis to this particular group, although I acknowledge the North American missionaries within their own countries (the US and Canada) historically and in the present (e.g. to Native Americans) and the many missionaries from other countries around the world. South Korea, for example, is the world's second-largest (after the US) missionary-sending nation, and may soon surpass the US in this regard (Moll, 2006). Second, the main focus of the memoirs, or at least of a substantial part of the books, had to be those MK experiences, and to a lesser extent, the subsequent influence of the MK experiences on the authors' later lives. I found these memoirs through searches of databases, online searches, and personal and Facebook requests for suggestions from friends and acquaintances, especially those who were, like me, alumni of Kodaikanal School in India. I also found a few books *about* MKs; these were generally not scholarly, but rather books of advice, often from authors associated with missionary work themselves, such as former missionaries, church leaders, consultants and psychologists (e.g. Danielson, 1984; Gray, 1995; Viser, 1986); these books gave me insights into the experiences of MKs and into how those experiences were perceived by others.

As stated earlier, the memoirists' experiences as MKs in other countries took place throughout the 20th century, with most of their experiences abroad clustered between the 1930s and the 1970s. Characteristics of the book-length memoirs studied for this project include the following:

(1) They were published between 1975 (Reimer) and 2014 (Gray, Hustad, Kopp), but predominantly in the 1990s and the early 2000s.
(2) The authors were (except for Kuegler) originally from the US or Canada.
(3) The authors were born between 1900 and 1979, with a fairly even distribution of births across the first six decades of the 20th century, and only six birth dates in the 1960s and 1970s. (Note that in a few cases the authors' birth years or ages were never explicitly given, so I had to ascertain them, at least roughly, by deduction from other dates and clues provided in the memoirs, such as ages at entering school, graduation dates and correlation with world events.)
(4) The authors were between the ages of 22 (a definite outlier) and 90 at the time of publication of their memoirs, with the majority of them between 40 and 80. I sensed that one cluster of authors were writing during the mid-life re-evaluation that often happens in one's forties, as a sort of self-assessment and even therapy, and that a second grouping felt as they neared the end of life, in their seventies and eighties, that they wanted to record their experiences for their families and for posterity, and possibly for a kind of 'closure' for themselves.
(5) The authors lived as MKs in a total of 26 countries outside of their home countries: Angola, Brazil, Cambodia, Cameroun, China, Costa Rica, Ethiopia, Guatemala, India, Indonesia, Ivory Coast, Kenya, Laos, Madagascar, Mexico, Netherlands Antilles, New Guinea, Nigeria, Pakistan, Philippines, Swaziland, Taiwan, Upper Volta, Venezuela, Vietnam and Zambia. (Note that some of the authors lived in more than one country as MKs; note also that the names of these countries are listed here as the authors gave them,

which were the names of the countries at the time the memoirists lived there, and I have not changed spellings or inserted new/changed names of any countries.)
(6) Twenty-two authors are female; 20 are male.
(7) Some of the MKs became missionaries themselves in later life (thus the highlighting of their roles as missionaries in some memoirs and their titles).
(8) The books were published by a wide range of publishers, from major commercial presses such as Penguin and Houghton Mifflin, to university presses such as University of Georgia and University of Virginia, to religious presses such as Zondervan and Nazarene, to many very small presses; in addition, several memoirs were self-published.
(9) The style and quality of the writing varied widely. Some of it was polished and professional, in a few cases written by academics (e.g. Braaten, Smith, Orr) and professional writers (e.g. Alter). At the other end of the spectrum, some of the writing was clearly amateurish and did not seem to have received the benefit of any kind of professional editing (e.g. Friesen).
(10) In a few cases, authors of more than one memoir attended the same schools; these schools included Bingham Academy in Ethiopia (three authors); Dalat School, Vietnam (two authors); Kodaikanal School, India (three authors); Murree Christian School, Pakistan (two authors); Shanghai American School (two authors); and Woodstock School, India (four authors). A few memoirists even attended the same school at the same time and knew each other (e.g. Bascom and Coleman, who were close friends at Bingham Academy; Addleton and Seaman, whose times at Murree Christian School overlapped). (Note that (a) a few authors attended more than one school; (b) names of schools were not always provided; (c) some students were homeschooled; correspondence courses were common. Note too that some of the books were vague about dates, sometimes not including such basic facts as the years that their families were in the mission field, their own dates of birth and when they attended certain schools.) See Table 2.1 for a summary of the main points of information about the memoirists.

The analysis

This analysis is a type of qualitative research that blends elements of literary analysis, feminist research and narrative inquiry. It is literary in

Table 2.1 'Missionary kid' memoirs

Author (year of publication)	Title	Gender	Countries lived in as MK
Addleton, J. (1997)	Some Far and Distant Place	Male	Pakistan
Alter, S. (1998)	All the Way to Heaven: An American Boyhood in the Himalayas	Male	India
Bascom, T. (2006)	Chameleon Days: An American Boyhood in Ethiopia	Male	Ethiopia
Braaten, C.E. (2010)	Because of Christ: Memoirs of a Lutheran Theologian	Male	Madagascar
Brush, S.E. (1998)	Farewell the Winterline: Memories of a Boyhood in India	Male	India
Coleman, D. (2003)	The Scent of Eucalyptus: A Missionary Childhood in Ethiopia	Male	Ethiopia
Cordell, R. (2008)	A Missionary's Daughter in India: The Autobiography of Ruth Cordell	Female	India
Dawson, M. (2009)	Growing Up Yanomamo: Missionary Adventures in The American Rainforest	Male	Venezuela
Denton, J. (2003)	Foreign Devil Boy or Older Brother?: A Missionary Kid's Experiences of Life in the Orient	Male	Hong Kong, China, Philippines
Deters, G. (2009)	Divine Betrayal: An Inspirational Story of Love, Rebellion and Redemption	Female	Brazil
Dilley, A.P. (2012)	Faith and Other Flat Tires: Searching for God on the Rough Road of Doubt	Female	Kenya
Espey, J. (1994)	Minor Heresies, Major Departures: A China Mission Boyhood	Male	China
Frerichs, C.E. (2010)	Desires of the Heart: A Daughter Remembers Her Missionary Parents	Female	Papua New Guinea
Friesen, P.R. (2003)	Ultimate Sacrifice: An Intimate Look into Missionary Boarding Schools and the Ultimate Sacrifice of Children	Male	Mali
Gray, L (2014)	Three Ring Circus: Life As a Missionary Kid in a Family of 11	Male	Philippines
Harrison, H.B. (1983)	From M.K. to R.M.	Female	Brazil
Harvey, V.P. (2009)	The Missionary Myth: Through the Eyes of a Missionary Kid	Female	Ivory Coast

Henderson-James, N. (2009)	At Home Abroad: An American Girl in Africa	Female	Angola
Hustad, M. (2014)	More than Conquerors: A Memoir of Lost Arguments	Female	The Netherlands Antilles
Jacoby, M.L.M. (2011)	Mish Kid to Mystic: Memoirs of a Missionary Daughter	Female	Cameroun
Kopp, D.A. (2014)	Made in Africa	Male	Zambia
Kuegler, S. (2005)	Child of the Jungle: The True Story of a Girl Caught Between Two Worlds	Female	Indonesia
Littell, J.F. (1995)	A Lifetime in Every Moment	Male	China
Lloret, D.B. (2004)	mk.cam: Tales from the Life of an Urban Missionary Kid	Male	Mexico, Costa Rica, Guatemala
Looper, E.H. (2008)	Under His Wings: Memoirs of a West African Missionary Kid	Female	Upper Volta
Maybury, H.C. (2011)	For the Souls and Soils of India: From Ohio Farm Land to the Mission Fields of India	Female	India
McMurdie, J.M. (2009)	Land of the Morning: A Civilian Internee's Poignant Memories of Sunshine and Shadows	Female	Philippines
Noyes, H. (1989)	China Born: Adventures of a Maverick Bookman	Male	China
Orr, E.N. (2003)	Gods of Noonday: A White Girl's African Life	Female	Nigeria
Peters, D.B. (1996)	Through Isaac's Eyes: Crossing of Cultures, Coming of Age, and the Bond Between Father and Son	Male	Vietnam
Phemister, M.A. (2009)	Lessons from a Broken Chopstick: A Memoir of a Peculiar Childhood	Female	Vietnam, Taiwan, Cambodia
Reimer, H.S. (1975)	A Growing Plant: Reflections of an 'M.K.' (Missionary's Kid)	Female	Swaziland
Schmitthenner, S. (2004)	Ramblings with Ruth	Male	India
Schoonmaker, P. (2011)	Mish-kid Mosaic	Male	India

(Continued)

Table 2.1 (continued) 'Missionary kid' memoirs

Author (year of publication)	Title	Gender	Countries lived in as MK
Schroeder, J.H. (2013)	Under an African Sky: The Unusual Life of a Missionaries' Kid in Ethiopia	Female	Ethiopia
Schroth, G.H. (2011)	Curry, Corduroy and the Call: A Mennonite Missionary's Daughter Grows up in Rural India	Female	India
Seaman, P.A. (1997)	Paper Airplanes in the Himalayas: The Unfinished Path Home	Male	Pakistan
Smith, H. (2010)	Tales of Wonder: Adventures Chasing the Divine	Male	China
Terry, R.J. (2011)	Help Me Be a Good Girl Amen: My Journey from Misionary Kid to Truth	Female	China
Van Reken, R.E. (1988)	Letters Never Sent	Female	Nigeria
Van Walkenburg, C.T. (2014)	37 Blessings of Growing Up as a Missionary Kid: The Lord Saves Those Crushed in Spirit	Female	Laos
Wiebe, V.B. (1990)	Sepia Prints: Memoirs of a Missionary in India	Female	India

the sense of looking for themes in written works that are a type of literature. It is feminist in the sense of examining power disparities (Lichtman, 2006: 163). It is also, clearly, a type of narrative inquiry; note Barkhuizen's (2013: 8) definition of narrative inquiry as 'research with aims of learning about the content of the experiences of the participants and their reflections of these'.

As I read and re-read the memoirs, I looked for themes that were related to colonialism and coloniality. As stated at the end of Chapter 1, I narrowed these themes to a list of six. I marked and copied passages that seemed to reflect these six themes. I knew I wanted to quote liberally from the memoirs, to give readers a strong and deep sense of the lives of these MKs, as well as of the ways in which their lives and their portrayals of their lives in the memoirs, shed light on the themes and in general on the colonial aspects of missionary work. So I carefully went through the memoirs again and again with the six themes in mind, selecting and marking passages related to the themes.

Throughout, I had to be, and was, very aware of my own positionality as I carried out this research. I was, as stated earlier, and am (because one's MK identity applies not only during the MK years but for life), an MK myself. I found myself identifying closely with some of the MKs, less so with others. I had some personal reactions, both positive and negative, to their stories and the attitudes they displayed. I remembered, though, that in some cases my attitudes and behaviors were similar to theirs, even if I prefer not to acknowledge the more negative ones now. Furthermore, I had to remind myself of historical changes that had taken place both before and after my own years in India. I also had to remind myself that my years as an academic, my commitment to certain progressive beliefs both in my academic work and in my personal life, and other personal characteristics and experiences all influenced the way I viewed the memoirs. I understand that my own experiences shaped the way I read and experienced these MK memoirs, whether I chose for them to do so or not. I understand too that this could have some potential to be a negative factor; on the other hand, I also think that my experiences may enrich and complexify my understandings of the memoirs, and of the memoirists' experiences and feelings. In a sense I am both an insider and an outsider; I can provide both emic and etic perspectives and approaches. I am using the memoirs as my data, and focusing on their words and ideas, yet I bring to this research not only my own background as a fellow MK but also certain theories and approaches based on my academic training and experience. A statement that has been helpful to me as I try to balance these factors is as follows:

> A researcher has ... a professional duty, to do a 'novel reading', an apt expression coined by Marjorie DeVault (1990): an interpretation by a person who is not socialized into the same system of meaning as the narrator but is familiar enough with it to recognize it as such. (Czarniawska, 2004: 62)

Yes, to a certain extent, I was 'socialized into the same system of meaning' as the writers of the memoirs, but I am also a person who has moved away from that system of meaning over a period of decades; I have also developed the distance provided by my identity as an academic and a scholar, as well as by further life experience over the decades since my living in India as an MK. I hope that I am able to balance these 'insider' and 'outsider' identities here, although I know very well that such balance is never 100% possible.

3 The Exotic

The most common terms used by the memoirists, and by others of the 20th century, about the strange, fascinating, unusual and 'Other' experiences of missionaries (and other travelers) are 'Oriental' and 'exotic'. The terms 'The Orient' and 'Orientalism' were in the past considered acceptable in academe and elsewhere; in fact, Orientalism was an area of scholarly study. However, in 1978 the scholar and theorist of postcolonial studies Edward Said published a book titled *Orientalism*, arguing that Western views of the East were Eurocentric, patronizing, stereotypical, Othering and suggested the superiority of Western culture. The terms Orientalism and 'Orient' represented these negative, condescending views. Although to many, the term 'exotic' simply means 'unusual' or 'very different from what "we" are used to', Said, along with Homi Bhabha, Gayatri Spivak and other theorists, has taught us about the pitfalls of the terms and concepts of 'Orientalism' and 'the exotic'. These terms in effect define non-Western countries and cultures in terms of how they are different from Western countries and cultures. The terms set up an 'us' and 'them' binary. Non-Western cultures are thereby 'Othered', condescended to and demeaned by these concepts.

> The Orient was almost a European invention, and had been since antiquity a place of romance, exotic beings, haunting memories and landscapes, remarkable experiences ... The Orient is ... the place of Europe's greatest and richest and oldest colonies, the source of ... one of its deepest and most recurring images of the Other. (Said, 1995: 87)

Since then, Said's views have been widely accepted, at least in academe and related circles. He mainly spoke about Western views of Arab cultures, but his argument was soon generalized to Western views of all Middle Eastern and Asian cultures, and indirectly to African cultures as well. Pruitt (2005: 3) notes that the word 'Orient' was used by 19th-century North American evangelicals 'to represent the area of the world stretching from historical Palestine to China and encompassing a wide variety of religious cultures, including Judaism, Islam, Greek and Syrian

Christianity'. She points out the breathtakingly entitled aspect of this as follows: 'Nineteenth-century American Protestants somehow managed to collapse that vast region of the world into a unitary concept, the "Orient"'. Pruitt (2005: 4) further states that '"the Orient" was more of an idea – a Western idea – than it was a definable place'. Pennycook (1998) writes about the way the British often used the term and concept 'the exotic' in a negative way. He writes further of the way Westerners spoke and wrote about China in the 19th century, with a pejorative 'Orientalist' approach, and he says that '[c]rucial in this process was the arrival of British Protestant missionaries, with their condescending and negative views toward China' (Pennycook, 1998: 169). Of course, there have always been terms that were common at one time and then became less acceptable; other such terms related to missionary work include 'heathen' and 'pagan'. The latter, for example, was used in a Harvard University doctoral dissertation title: *Protestant America and the Pagan World* (Phillips, 1969).

These theoretical concepts are instantiated in everyday life in North America (and elsewhere in the West). For just one small example, I recently received in the mail a glossy brochure for Oceania Cruises titled 'Exotic Interludes'. The listed cruises included 'Pure Polynesia', 'Pearls & Moai' and 'Shimmering South Pacific', among others. Reinforcing the 'exotic' theme was one tour titled 'Opulent Orient'. Apparently the terms 'exotic' and 'Orient' are considered perfectly acceptable by many, and can even be used to entice tourists to part with their money in order to visit places that are, in the advertisements, framed as part of the mysterious East. One tour even includes a visit to a plantation.

Many American missionaries too, although they often spoke of how they loved the countries where they worked and lived, denigrated them as well, effectively exoticizing, Othering and looking down upon those countries all at once. In some ways typical was the example of Isaac Headland, an American missionary in China in the early 20th century, whose writings displayed a condescending and negative attitude toward China and Chinese people that was similar to those of the British missionaries. He wrote (Headland, 1912) of all the ways that, in his opinion, the Christian religion had brought progress to non-Christian countries around the world. As the US became more powerful in the 20th century, 'so too did the American missionaries and sinologists come to dominate the production of images of China' (Pennycook, 1998: 170), and those images were often stereotypical and negative. A few missionaries, especially missionary leaders and scholars, were also aware of issues of Othering, and there was discussion of these issues in missionary leadership conferences in Europe and the US. American missionary and author Daniel Johnson

Fleming, who was a missionary in India for 12 years and who wrote 30 books about missionary topics, wrote in the 1920s 'not only against the old-time vocabulary of conquest and condescension but against a subtler ethnocentrism that operated when one continued to speak of China or Japan as missionary lands, "as though being our parish abroad was their *raison d'etre*"' (quoted in Hutchison, 1987: 155). Fleming's attitude and understanding were not typical; he was ahead of his time. However, many American missionaries of the more liberal bent 'reduced the scope and intensity of "Orientalism"'; these 'missionary-influenced scholars and teachers of the post-World War II era long preceded Said and his followers in combatting negative and patronizing images of Asian peoples' (Hollinger, 2017: 292).

The memoirists in this study are not, with very few exceptions, academics, and so the term 'The Orient' is used unself-consciously by some; the most egregious case among these memoirs is author Denton's use of the phrase in his (sub)title (*A Missionary Kid's Experiences of Life in the Orient*). The word 'exotic' is also used by some memoirists. More common than the actual use of these terms are the attitudes conveyed by these words, 'Oriental' and, especially, 'exotic'.

How does the concept of the 'exotic' apply to the missionary enterprise? Missionaries (in the case of the memoirists' parents, North American missionaries) go to other countries, generally 'underdeveloped' or 'developing' countries (although those terms are problematic), to share their 'more advanced' knowledge in the areas of religion, education, medicine, government and more. As Johnston (2003) notes, the missionary career itself is regarded as 'exotic' (p. 8) and full of 'adventures' (p. 19). It is built into the missionary project that there are differences between their home countries and the countries where they do their mission work, and that although the differences can be interesting, even exciting, the ways of the non-Western countries are generally considered inferior by Westerners in general and missionaries in particular. 'Exotic' is perhaps a useful shorthand in this situation, because it points out the differences, and even appears to find them intriguing, but the problem is that at the same time the word implies that the differences are generally to the detriment of the countries where the missionaries work. Even the 'intriguing' descriptor sometimes implies difference in an Othering fashion.

It could be argued that missionaries were no different than their contemporaries in other fields (e.g. diplomats, businesspeople) in this tendency to emphasize the exotic aspects of the countries where they worked, and to an extent this is true. However, an added factor for missionaries is that characterizing the countries and people in their new locales as exotic can work as another justification for their (the missionaries') going to 'rescue' the poor 'native' or 'primitive' people from their ignorance, through, admirably in many people's eyes, bringing both Western civilization and Western religion (Christianity) to them. Thus the Otherizing that accompanies tropes of the exotic is complicit in the rationale for the missionary work itself.

Missionary kids also absorb some of this thinking, as children usually do absorb the views of their parents and other adults in their lives, and in their memoirs, they tend to offer examples of these differences. In their cases, they often think of the differences as exciting and remarkable. Whether or not they use the term 'exotic' (as Coleman, Hustad, Kopp, Looper and Schoonmaker do), the meaning is implied. Some (e.g. Van Walkenburg) use the term 'unusual' to mean the same thing. Schroeder (2013) even includes the word in her memoir's subtitle, *The Unusual Life of a Missionaries' Kid in Ethiopia*. Phemister (2009) includes the phrase 'a peculiar childhood' in her title. Others speak of their 'adventures' (e.g. Schroeder) and of 'dangerous journeys' (e.g. Terry). Van Valkenburg (2014: 14) opines that *Life as an MK was always an adventure*, and further states in an understandable and anodyne but rather shallow and self-congratulatory fashion, which is unfortunately quite representative of the low or rather almost non-existent level of analysis of many of the memoirs (but we should remember that very few of the writers, even as adults, are scholars or theorists), *We MKs have had the privilege of seeing so many interesting things and experiencing such a variety of unusual activities* (Van Valkenburg, 2014: 85). Buettner (2004: 63–64) tells us that many children of British colonials during the Raj were nostalgic for their days in India, and considered those years 'magical' and idyllic, because of the freedom the children had, and because of 'the warmth and brightness of Indian skies' as well as other signs of a more exotic life than could be found back in England. The other side of this feeling was, however, the difficulties of going home to England afterward; Buettner (2004: 63) reminds readers that the English writer Rumer Godden believed that going back to England marked 'the end of our childhood'. Again we see the commonalities between the lives of British colonials and those of missionaries, and in this case, between the lives of their children, enhanced by the romanticizing of the 'exotic'.

The memoirists seem to feel that books about growing up in different countries, especially non-Western countries, are a genre that should offer readers the excitement and even titillation in some cases of stories of the strange, the weird, the unusual, with the whiff of far-off worlds, almost as if they were writing articles for travel magazines. They also assume that readers will want to read about such exotic and unusual situations, and in fact this may well be true. Addleton (2000: 30), one of the memoirists studied here, writes in a different publication, a review of nine MK memoirs, that 'the exotic settings are clearly meant to help sell the books in question'. Accordingly, they make a point of emphasizing tales of features of the countries where they lived that differ from those at 'home', and of their 'adventures'. Those who lived in small villages, remote areas and/or jungles generally emphasized the exotic the most. Kuegler (2005), for example, who lived in jungle areas of Indonesia, portrays her life as if she lived like the 'natives' in very 'primitive' situations; her title, *Child of the Jungle*, clearly reveals her stance. She also writes with intense and even lyrical prose of how happy she was there, from the beginning. *I felt at home there, felt like this was the life I was born for, a life without stress in midst of nature, untouched by modern civilization* (Kuegler, 2005: 20). This love of the life in the jungle with the Fayu people seems to have been genuine, but does not preclude Kuegler's romanticizing and exoticizing the jungle and its residents, a long tradition in the West (Westerners could, it appears, simultaneously romanticize and condescend to non-Westerners with ease). Dawson's (2009) case, and self-presentation, is similar; his subtitle is *Missionary Adventures in the American Rainforest*. (By 'American', he means South American, specifically Venezuelan.) It is significant that the marketing matter and blurbs on the back of this book use the terms 'primitive Amazon jungle' and 'stone-age people', clearly knowing that readers are likely to be attracted to such exoticizing and Othering portrayals.

The MK memoirists, even though they are writing as adults, try to capture the ways in which the countries in which they grew up were full of difference. There is an artlessness about the way these facts, stories and ideas are included. We have to remember that these memoirs are written for information, entertainment and remembering, not as academic analysis. So when some of the MKs use the term 'exotic', or similar terms such as 'unusual' and 'adventures', they use them uncritically. A representative passage from the memoirs is the following from Kopp (2014), speaking of the Indian community in South Africa:

> *The Indians' attention to fabric and color and beauty was, to me, distinctly* other. *Where a village smelled like sweat, earth, grass and maize beer, the exotic smells of India joined a chaotic combination of spice, incense and dhal. I loved the smell of curry. Here the women wore their gold out loud and sometimes saris slipped to reveal trim brown midriffs or rolls of fat. The household idols sat squarely in their special places where a family focused their efforts to appease the angry gods, stave off disaster or curry favor. (Pun intended.)* (p. 109)

Kopp is describing his genuine appreciation for the sensory aspects of Indian life that he observes, but he speaks of it all as 'other' and exotic.

Below I discuss, and give examples of, the most common types of 'exotic' or 'unusual' features described in the memoirs, in roughly descending order of frequency of mention. (Since I use the words 'exotic' and 'unusual' extensively, from here on I stop putting quotation marks around the words, but readers can be assured that they are still implied.)

Animals

I write first about animals, because by far the most common examples of the exotic found in these memoirs are mentions of adventurous encounters with various animals such as snakes, tigers, leopards, elephants, monkeys, wild boar, hyenas, wolves, crocodiles, mongooses, Himalayan red bears, peacocks, scorpions, flying ants and driver ants. Perhaps this is because to many people animals almost epitomize the exotic. They provide the most vivid examples of difference, and of the romance of faraway lands; these are animals that most North Americans see only in zoos, or in movies about jungles and safaris in Asia and Africa. Another possible reason for the universal mentions of 'wild' and 'unusual' animals is that the animals do not raise issues of culture, religion or morality in the way that other examples of the exotic may do.

In any case, in almost every memoir, there are pages and pages, even whole chapters, on adventures with wild or 'strange' animals. Cordell (2008) includes a chapter on 'Animals in India' in her memoir, as does Coleman (2003) about animals in Ethiopia in his chapter 'Ferenjie Nature'. The animal mentioned most often is snakes, including varieties such as cobras, vipers, boa constrictors and anacondas. The next most frequent is tigers, and close behind, leopards. Wild animals are often mentioned in the contexts of exciting, close brushes with danger. Schroth (2011), for example, writes of finding a nine-foot snake curled up under her bed, and Deters (2009: 81) writes that *[o]ftentimes, I opened the outhouse door to greet a poisonous snake coiled lazily upon the dirt floor, or even the outhouse seat.* Kopp (2014) reminds readers of how deadly snakes can be, and that he and his family always kept their eyes on the path when walking. Looper (2008: 59) writes of the time that her family was on a car trip and *a lioness tried to charge us and Uncle Smith was able to shoot it.* Sadly, in a few cases, encounters with animals ended in the death of memoirists' acquaintances, as in the case of Kopp's friend who was caught and eaten by a crocodile. Looper (2008: 13) combines three of the oldest clichés ever about Africa with a mention of an exotic animal, as follows: *the isolation and the stillness of the nights were punctuated by the syncopated beat of African drums, or the grunting of lions hunting their prey.* Other memoirists too were prone to such clichés. Kopp (2014: 154), for example, writes of playing in the area near a lake, summarizing one day's adventures as *[j]ust our family and friends playing in wild, unspoiled Africa.*

I must admit that I myself, in my second publication on my MK background (Vandrick, 1999b), provided (at the request of the editor) photos of myself and other missionary kids of my acquaintance with exotic animals (a leopard, an elephant). I also have a small trove of often-told stories about cobras (the one that came up the drains in the bathroom when my little brother was about to bathe; the one that hung from the ceiling above my parents' bed), scorpions (the one that stung my mother on the foot on the verandah of our house), and, most dramatic of all, leopards (the one that caught and ate our pet dog). I am quite sure that each of the memoirists has her or his own similar collection of well-worn stories at the ready, even in addition to the ones included in the memoirs, as we are all sometimes asked 'what was it like to grow up in India/China/Kenya/Brazil?' and what people usually want to hear, it seems, is something dramatic and exotic.

Foods

Another favorite topic is that of exotic foods, new to the MKs. This is perhaps reminiscent of how most descriptions of most cultures, especially in non-academic writing or speaking, allude to the foods of different countries and areas. Returning tourists, for example, often recount their meals and the foods they ate during their travels; I certainly do this myself. This tendency is perhaps natural in view of the almost-universal human interest in food and eating, and in view of the fact that this topic, like that of animals, is non-controversial and brings people together. The emphasis on food is a marker of enjoyable difference. For these memoirists, writing about food is a simple, obvious way to show the differences they encountered, in an almost 'can you top this?' tone. Littell (1995) writes of such unusual, for him, Chinese foods as sea slugs, jellyfish skins and coagulated pigs' blood. Kuegler (2005), in jungle areas of Indonesia, tells of foods eaten there such as crocodile, grilled bat wings and grubs. Jacoby (2011) describes favorite foods in Cameroun: fried plantain bananas rolled into pinwheels, slabs of fried breadfruit and crispy eggplant, bowls of pawpaw melons filled with fruit such as fresh coconut chunks. Henderson-James (2009) writes of eating flying ants in Angola. Finally, Looper (2008) notes the eating of rats, grasshoppers and termites in Upper Volta. All of these stories and lists are recounted as eager offerings to the readers' anticipated expectations (with a *frisson*) of unusual, even sometimes disgusting details about the strange and faraway lands where the MKs lived.

Appearances and Behaviors of Local People

Local people are sometimes described as exotic in their appearances or behaviors. Regarding appearance, for example, Kuegler (2005) has an entire chapter emphasizing how primitive the Fayu people of West Papua, Indonesia are, saying that they are *wild-looking* and noting that many are *completely naked*, with bones through their noses (Kuegler, 2005: 16). Looper writes of an old man whose ear lobes were stretched out by having worn heavy earrings; *now they sagged to his shoulders and he amused the children in his group by putting his arm up through the hole in one of his ear lobes* (p. 71). Nakedness or semi-nakedness is a recurring theme. Women's public bare-breastedness in New Guinea is noted with surprise by Frerichs, and Kuegler remarks that Fayu women sometimes breastfed dingo puppies or even piglets. Looper describes a woman who welcomed her and her family;

> *when she heard we had arrived, she came running to meet us, bare to the waist with her old, withered breasts flapping as she ran. Six or seven half-naked boys and girls followed her, and she proudly told us they were her grandkids.* (Kuegler, 2005: 69)

Looper writes further regarding public nakedness as she tells of people relieving themselves at the side of a road or against the side of a convenient building.

Schoonmaker vividly describes the appearance of a beggar as follows:

> *It was entirely naked, squatting and sifting through a filthy open Indian town gutter, searching for whatever piece of refuse might still be edible – a rotten orange or banana peel, a soggy cob of corn picked clean, some scrap of fetid food thrown into the drain by a bazaar vendor. I still couldn't tell if it was a man or a woman – the chest was too shrunken, the limbs too shriveled, the torso too emaciated, the lice-eaten hair too matted, the face too expressionless.* (Schoonmaker, 2011: 36)

Addleton (1997) writes of seeing, at a local fair in Pakistan, *hijiras* (male-to-female transsexuals in India and Pakistan). Henderson-James (2009) writes of drumming and singing. Regarding behaviors, the most dramatic examples are mentions of local people's being cannibals (Kuegler (2005), speaking of the jungles of Indonesia, and Frerichs (2010), writing of New Guinea). Frerichs mentions a topic almost equally shocking to Westerners:

polygamy. Sometimes the MKs would tell each other frightening but enjoyable stories (in the tradition of children's scary stories everywhere) about dacoits and ransoms. *We heard stories about Teli wallahs, who would kidnap children and drill holes in their skulls, hang them over a fire, and drain the precious oil from their bodies* (Alter, 1998: 98). The point here is not that these descriptions are untrue (although obviously some are), but that the memoirists choose to emphasize and 'play up' these exotic (to them) appearances and behaviors.

Stereotypes and unconscious racism about local people sometimes appear, as in Gray's writing in a chapter tellingly titled 'Outsiders'. He writes that when his family arrived in the Philippines, *dark-skinned figures were everywhere* (Gray, 2014: 1). He further writes about his first impressions of the Philippines as noisy, humid and chaotic. Later he alludes to witch doctors and *demon-possessed* people (p. 49). And he describes Filipina girls as having *slanted eyes* (p. 112). Denton (2003: 121) too writes about the Philippines and mentions that witchcraft was *still a common practice ... in the remote villages* when he was there. Looper (2008: 65) also writes of meeting an African couple: *when they saw me, their round, black faces lit up with broad grins.* The words she uses, although unintentionally so, remind us of common tropes used about North American black people and their appearances, starting in the days of slavery and continuing into the present. Some of these descriptions may be true, but the point is the way the memoirists highlight the aspects of appearances and other factors that were the most unfamiliar and, yes, exotic, to their North American eyes and ears.

Ceremonies and Rituals

Occasionally the MKs, by happenstance or on purpose, witnessed local ceremonies and rituals, whether religious or cultural or some combination thereof. Orr (2003: 228), for example, once saw in Nigeria *the initiation of boys into manhood*, including being lashed on their backs until they bled. Schoonmaker (2011) writes in detail about Hindu rituals in which people are pierced through the tongue and other body parts. Looper (2008) tells of blood sacrifices, as well as amulets and fetishes, related to religion in West Africa. Bascom (2006) writes of goats being sacrificed to the tree gods. All of these were, clearly, dramatic events in the lives of the MKs. Like children everywhere (in this case, adults telling about childhood events), the memoirists write about the events with a mixture of intrigue and repulsion. They clearly enjoy telling the stories, imagining how readers will react.

Illnesses

Many of the memoirists also write of illnesses, especially tropical or other illnesses unlikely to be encountered 'back home'. In some cases, they seem to write with a certain amount of relish about the repellent details of the diseases. They write of observing, and in some cases contracting, malaria, tuberculosis and leprosy. Kuegler devotes a whole chapter to 'Malaria and Other Diseases'. However, the memoirists write with particular relish, clearly hoping to shock and even disgust readers (in an enjoyable way!) about worms (ringworms, pinworms, roundworms) and other parasites that invade the human body. Harrison (1983: 18) writes with a note of childlike glee of family members who, after returning from Brazil to the US for a furlough, discover that they have *intestinal parasites – four varieties of them!* Deters (2009) got roundworms and pinworms. In a particularly graphic description, she tells of being given castor oil for roundworms: *After a few hours, the worms began to expel themselves from my body by the dozens, or maybe even hundreds. Ugly, round, white worms, squirming loosely from my bowels* (Deters, 2009: 139). Deters seems to enjoy passing on such descriptions, as she also writes about another occasion when her father had to pull *little bugs out from the soles of my feet* (p. 130).

Geography

A frequent topic is the beauty but also the ruggedness of the land, the primitive transportation and infrastructure, and the difficulties of travel. Seaman (1997) writes of taking train trips through vast deserts, and of the severe beauty of the landscape. Kopp (2014: 154) speaks of *wild, unspoiled Africa*. Several memoirists write of the lack of good roads and easy transportation, which makes for difficult but in many cases exciting, even exhilarating trips and experiences. Several of the male MKs (e.g. Bascom) write with obvious pleasure of trips on rough roads or paths through the jungle in Jeeps or other hardy vehicles, and of fording rushing rivers. Jacoby recounts crossing rivers on small boats that had to be poled or paddled.

Hardships

There are also tales of various hardships, generally told in tones of pride at withstanding such conditions. Some of the tales are reminiscent of American stories of 19th century 'pioneer days' on the vast prairies of the US, mainly because the memoirists often use similar language and imagery. They write that transportation was (as mentioned above) long and difficult, and that electricity and running water were sometimes erratic or in short supply. Kopp (2014: 5) remembers that in 'the bush' electricity was provided by a generator for three hours a day, and that

> *[e]verything in the bush was more work. Kerosene for lamps had to be brought in from town. Water was pumped from the river, stored and purified. Basic food stuffs were transported from town or raised in the back yard. Bread had to be baked. Most everyone kept chickens ... Laundry, hot water, cooking, cleaning – all happened without external power.*

They reminisce about times when they felt afraid or in danger. Deters (2009: 218) writes that a church service in a new place was disrupted by *a large group of rough and tumble men* and she *was terrified. This uncivilized area was not unlike the American Wild West in the late 1800s, with weekly shootings and a general sense of lawlessness.*

The memoirists' comments about all these matters and areas of difference described above, whether labeled as exotic or unusual or simply described for the readers' enjoyment of the strange and wonderful adventures experienced by the MKs, often show a little unconscious superiority and presumptuous smugness. For example, Lloret (2004: 13) says *it did not take long for me to learn the ways of native customs.*

Lasting Effects

The MKs' attitudes toward the exotic, or at least their need to emphasize differences that they saw as exotic, are perhaps most dramatically and floridly, but not untypically, expressed by Schoonmaker (2011: 24), as follows:

> *It was scenes such as these that India unremittingly engraved into my developing psyche year after indelible year – the common expected juxtaposition of vast extremes – of the inviolably sacred and contemptuously profane, the ravishingly beautiful and abhorrently awful, the rapturously ecstatic and revoltingly hideous, the inenarrably ineffable and prosaically mundane, the singularly aesthetical and abominably odious, the unassailably rational and fantastically absurd.*

I must note that very occasionally, one of the memoirists shows an awareness of the problematic nature of looking at the local people and customs as exotic. Addleton (1997: 103) writes that *[t]he bizarre and sometimes cruel displays [at a fair] both fascinated and repelled me.* He adds, making an insightful comparison, that

> [a]t the worst of times, I imagined that I was part of a larger circus, that we missionary children were also on display, whether living as foreigners with our parents in Pakistan or accompanying them on their occasional visits to raise financial support in churches back in America. (p. 103)

He sees that there are always multiple sides to any perceptions, and that where one stands influences how one regards the behavior of the 'Other'. In effect, he is asking the question of who is exotic to whom. He further describes with embarrassment *[t]he missionary family, dressed in native costume* (Addleton, 1997: 112) on deputations to churches back in the US during furloughs. He sees that missionaries are both looking at Others as exotic and exploiting that exoticism to fund their missionary work, in the meanwhile catching a small (although not, of course, fully comparable) glimpse of the consequences of such Otherizing.

Discourses of the exotic and of the Orient in these memoirs are generally employed out of innocence and naiveté, but nonetheless are complicit in the Othering of non-Western people and cultures, something one can note without necessarily assigning blame, but also without ignoring the implications. They are another reminder of the colonial roots of the missionary enterprise, and of the ways in which the missionaries and their children were enmeshed in colonial (and sometimes racist, although generally not consciously so) attitudes and practices.

4 Treatment of Local People

Condescension, Criticism and Mocking of Local People

Missionary kids, like their parents and mission boards, were used to thinking of themselves and their families as superior, the ones bringing the true religion and culture to the 'natives'; consciously or unconsciously, they treated local people, such as the servants in their homes, as inferior. This sense of superiority is of course not unique to missionaries. As noted throughout this book, it echoes and is in some senses part of the colonial movement and residual coloniality, and reflects racism worldwide as well.

A larger group of which missionaries are in some ways a part is that of expatriates (commonly dubbed 'expats'), and some of them exemplify condescending attitudes shown to local people. The term expatriate refers to those (usually white, from Western countries) who live a good portion of their lives in another country; these are not generally immigrants, but long-term visitors. Typifying many (although of course not all) expats' attitudes, the novelist Joseph O'Neill, in his novel *The Dog* (2014), writes about how expats in Dubai display 'bossiness and haughtiness' toward local, especially non-white, people (often immigrants from poorer countries) in roles such as waiters and servants. He quotes other expats from a computer listserv thread as referring to 'the imbecilities of the servant class' (O'Neill, 2014: 112) and providing such examples as the following: 'I got one. Our cleaning lady whose [sic] from Indonesia and a very nice young lady, put away some books with the spines facing INSIDE'. 'Think I can beat that. I was at Starbucks yesterday and the Indian gentleman waiter tried to "tidy away" the newspaper I was reading. He had no idea that the whole point of sitting down was to read the newspaper. He didn't know what reading a newspaper was!' 'Try explaining that L socks go with R socks! Never works. They always think L goes with L because it looks the same. Drives me potty' (O'Neill, 2014: 112). These examples of condescending mockery are painful to read, but not unrepresentative, perhaps, of the way some expats, influenced by the tradition of colonialism and by conscious or unconscious racism and classism, think and talk about local people, especially those with jobs as servants. In addition to being racist, living in someone else's country and then critiquing and mocking the local residents is disrespectful and rude.

Unfortunately, some of the comments made by the MK memoirists about local people and especially servants are very similar to these expat remarks listed by O'Neill. In the memoirists' case, the comments arise from being creatures of the time period (mainly the middle of the 20th century), and in particular from being part of the European/North American colonial tradition. The British rule and influence in India are perhaps the most prominent (or at least the most often and fully described) example of this tradition. We are all familiar with images of the white British government, military and business people (largely men, but often with wives, daughters and other females living in their households and active in their societies) who are surrounded by Indian servants, guards, soldiers and associates, almost always clearly at a lower level of status. However, these historical reasons are not excuses.

Some of these images persist to this day, in England, the Commonwealth countries and the US in particular, in novels, films and television shows. In a recent example, there has been a television show on the Public Broadcasting System's Masterpiece series, called *Indian Summers* (Rutnam, 2015), set in 1932 in the 'hill station' (cities in the hills of Asian countries, especially India, where the British went to escape the heat of the plains) of Simla. This television show portrays the interactions of the British and the Indians in the government and military, including those active in the independence movement. It illustrates that the British were often condescending to and dismissive of Indians, even those who had risen to high positions. Even the British who were polite in public were often much less so in private. Examples of novels about the period of the Raj, especially the period approaching Independence, include Paul Scott's *The Raj Quartet* (1976) and his follow up novel *Staying On* (1998), which with their vast casts of characters, British and Indian, showed the complex and very colonial-inflected interactions among them. *The Raj Quartet* was later made into a television mini-series titled (after the first of the four novels) *The Jewel in the Crown* (Morahan et al., 1984). Other novels depicting interactions between the British and the Indians include E.M. Forster's famous *A Passage to India* (1952) and M.M. Kaye's *The Far Pavilions* (1978/1997). Some of the famed Merchant Ivory films, especially those based on the novels of Ruth Prawer Jhabvala (e.g. *Heat and Dust*, 1975) also deal at least partially with the Raj years.

There are many other examples of novels, films and television shows, as well as those about the colonial days in other countries (besides India), such as some countries in Africa. Perhaps the most well-known of novels of outsiders about Africa, historically, is Joseph Conrad's *Heart of Darkness* (1899). Other European-authored works on colonial periods in Asia and Africa include George Orwell's semi-autobiographical *Burmese Days* (1934), about his time in Burma during the later days of British colonial rule there, and Isak Dinesen's *Out of Africa* (1937), about her experience as a colonial in Kenya. Note that all of the books, films and television shows discussed here are by British and other European authors, which means that these accounts (fictional and otherwise) are naturally at least somewhat biased toward the European/colonial viewpoint, a perspective echoed by North Americans. In these books and other media, without exception, there are distressing portrayals of the treatment of local people by the European colonists. This does not necessarily mean that the authors themselves agreed with these types of behaviors, but they swam in those seas, and their work reflected their own experiences and observations.

Scholarly work too finds that missionaries also often made pejorative remarks about their servants, although they heavily depended on those servants. Hunter quotes the writings of a female missionary in China as follows: '[I]t is almost more work to keep after them than to do the things one's self' (Hunter, 1984: 160). Another letter writer in Hunter's study wrote of her sewing woman that '[s]he has the peculiar strong odor about her that most of them have. When we are out we fear she will use our combs and toothbrushes, we tried for a while to keep them hid, but just cant [sic] all the time' (Hunter, 1984: 163).

Books by writers who are actually from the colonized countries present other viewpoints, of course. They often describe similar behaviors of the colonizers but from a clearly more critical point of view. Prominent examples of such books are Nigerian author Chinua Achebe's *Things Fall Apart* (1958), Zimbabwean writer Tsitsi Dangarembga's *Nervous Conditions* (2004) and Indian author Amitav Ghosh's *Sea of Poppies* (2008), all novels. Most of these and other books by local authors born and raised in Asia and Africa did not appear in Western countries until the 1960s and, especially, the 1970s and 1980s, finally giving wider voice to the actual citizens of their countries as opposed to the voices of those from Europe and North America.

The Memoirists' Stereotypes, Conscious and Unconscious

Turning to the contents of the memoirs in this study, we find that the MKs (sometimes quoting their parents) have a variety of ways of referring to the local people, some positive and some negative and demeaning, and almost all influenced by colonial traditions and customs. Frerichs, for example, says that *Europeans customarily referred to New Guinean adults as 'boys' and 'girls'* (Frerichs, 2010: 89). This practice is, of course, one that North Americans will recognize as the demeaning way that African Americans were often referred to by many, from the days of enslaved people up until the recent past (and, most unfortunately, sometimes in the present). Stereotypes are frequently in evidence. The memoirists often display a common one, one which on some level they believe redounds to their own credit: the idea that they loved and were loved by the local people. Tropes about the close relationships between the missionary families and the local people were fervently believed in. This was particularly true when discussing servants, about whom more below.

There are plenty of such statements about relationships with the local people in general that convey a genuine belief of a deep connection to the country, culture and people of the area where the missionaries live. There are many claims, or rather assumptions, that the local people are very happy to have the missionaries there. As Van Valkenburg (2014: 78) says, *In my mind I never felt any different from the Laotians*, and she assumes the Lao people felt the same about her. Similarly, Maybury (2011: 152) quotes her father's letter that says *The response of the Islampur people is a continual joy and satisfaction. In a most unusual way they have accepted us. We are no longer foreigners in Islampur. We are part of the town. Our joys are theirs, our sorrows are theirs.* These claims seem presumptuous, although of course we cannot definitively know the truth of the matter. Johnston (2017: ix), in his research on evangelical teaching of English in Poland, mentions the vivid term 'false-bottomed friendships', in which those with less power are concerned that their friendship is being cultivated for the 'ulterior goal of conversion and integration into the local evangelical community'. This situation can bring about the result that local people feel resentful but don't feel they can protest. The situation may or may not be applicable in the cases of Maybury's family and other MK memoirists, but there are some resonances with the descriptions in the memoirs.

Although the memoirists' statements about their relationships with local people come across as genuine and heartfelt, and the statements are probably sometimes somewhat accurate on an individual level, one cannot help but wonder if the local people always felt the same way as the missionaries and their children did. What, for example, is one to make of Kopp's statement about a local Zambian couple that *Mama and Papa Lubwika (Zambian) served as surrogate grandparents. Their love extended beyond the irrelevancies of race, color and ethnicity* (Kopp, 2014: 159). The phrase 'the irrelevancies of race, color and ethnicity' sounds oblivious to anyone reading this with any sense of the history and pervasiveness of racial issues everywhere, and especially in colonial contexts, which are contexts of unequal power. The certainty that missionaries felt in the rightness of their religion, and of their quest to spread their religion, inspired such statements as the following by Schroth (2011: 19): *The People, as Dad terms the multitudes, have greeted us joyfully, garlanded our necks, and now wait expectantly for increased blessings from God by way of this Missionary.* (Note the capitalization of the word 'missionary'.) These images of mutual connection, respect and even love between missionaries and local people were clearly important to the missionaries and their children to believe, and they had a stake, both emotional and religious, in continuing to believe in these images and relationships. Questioning them would undermine the significance of the missionary enterprise, and on a larger, contextual level, the colonial enterprise. It would be too painful to doubt or question these beliefs.

Sense of Superiority

Although probably not purposefully or consciously, many of the MK portrayals of the local people project notes of superiority and of condescension. For example, Harvey (2009: 139) states that her mother often exclaimed *Those savages* when *she was annoyed at something done by one of her African neighbors or even by our young house girl, Nyinge.* Hustad (2014: 44) asserts that *[t]he natives of Bonaire were superstitious*, and continues by saying that the natives often said *'no problem'*, and that some of her parents' colleagues saw *no problem as indicative of a Caribbean-style laziness or apathy.*

Even when appearing to speak respectfully about local people, missionaries and their children are often condescending. As noted above, Schroth's father called Indians 'The People'; he would say, *God sent us here to save 'The People'*, or direct a servant to *[g]ather the people for a meeting* (Schroth, 2011: 92). Similarly, Maybury's father remarks, *We hope to have a pilau dinner to celebrate the occasion with the Indians* (Maybury, 2011: 154). This wording ('the People' or 'the Indians') is reminiscent of the use of the terms 'the Negroes' or 'the blacks' in the US, terms that are commonly recognized (because of the way they were used by whites) to be demeaning and dehumanizing.

Harvey shows a little insight about this sense of superiority displayed by missionaries toward and about local people: *The European* [by which she seems to mean 'white Westerner'] *missionary comes with a conversion agenda. All too often, he or she puts aside the customs of the target population and degrades them as heathen. The missionary sets their own culture and theology on a higher plane* (Harvey, 2009: 139–140).

Treatment of Servants

The most frequent local people mentioned in the memoirs, especially in terms of the MKs' relationships with local people, are servants. Like other colonials, almost all missionaries had servants. From the early days of the missionary enterprise, there was some ambivalence about having servants, and about the servants themselves. Baller (1907: 72) begins with lofty statements about servants, saying 'It is a great thing to have a devoted servant. How do you secure this? … Love your servant and seek the highest good'. He goes on to remind the reader that missionaries themselves are servants, in their case servants of God. However, Baller then rather spoils the high-flown positive thoughts just quoted when he continues by saying, 'It is not easy to lick raw men into shape. And when you have had all your trouble, you may find that the material scarcely pays the labor' (Baller, 1907: 72). This pivot to the negative and dehumanizing view of servants as 'raw men' who need licking into shape, and as 'material', in counterpoint to Baller's lofty first quotation, captures something about the mixed feelings and the stereotypical thinking that some missionaries and their children have displayed ever since, including in the memoirs in this study.

As with their feelings about other local people, missionary families usually liked to think that there was a close, almost familial, relationship between the families and their servants. Espey (1994: 43) claims that *[t]he cook and the amah were naturally members of the household as essential to its unity as ourselves.* There is a particularly complex situation when local people work regularly in the missionaries' homes and surroundings. Cooks, maids, nannies, gardeners, chauffeurs and handymen are both omnipresent and invisible. They are paid; it is a job; yet there is a sense that the relationship between employer and employee is more intimate than most job relationships. Servants see missionaries in the private interiors of their homes and tend to their needs for food, water, clean clothes, clean bathrooms and bedrooms, and childcare. Sometimes there was a discomfort with the intimacy of this close daily connection, which could include the servants' doing such personal tasks as suckling children and washing infirm adults (Cleall, 2012). Although the discomfort was rarely mentioned explicitly in the MK memoirs, readers can pick up clues of such feelings in some cases. Schroth, for example, lists servant tasks rather graphically and with a hint of distaste (at least about the chamber pots):

> *[I]n order to be free to Do God's Work, missionaries' households require a cook, a mali to tend the garden, a man to draw water from the well, and a sweeper, the woman who sweeps the house and empties our chamber pots twice a day.* (Schroth, 2011: 23)

In many ways, servants know more about the missionary families than many of their fellow missionaries or other friends know. Yet it is mostly a very lopsided intimacy, in that one participant has most of the power, and the other is dependent on the first for her or his livelihood. I believe there was and is often genuine affection between the missionaries and their servants. Furthermore, the employer needs the servant's services, and the servant needs the wages earned. Nevertheless, it is still an unequal relationship. Despite this, the missionaries and in particular the MKs, at least as shown in the memoirs, seemed to have a stake in believing that they and the servants were very close, and that the servants were practically members of the family. Terry (2011: 118), for example, says of a later-in-life visit to her family's former servants, that the servants *had enjoyed our visit as much as we did ... They held our hands in both of theirs, bowed and grinned.* This statement is almost painful in its presumption of similar feelings. Equally distressing are the words 'bowed and grinned', with their echoes of behaviors that colonized people, as well as racially oppressed people, have so often had to display. I don't mean to equate the lives of servants to missionaries with those of slaves, but there is a commonality of coping strategies used by oppressed peoples. Similarly, when Looper and her family went back to visit their old missionary locale, she writes that their former houseboy Boanga and his wife Dadodiya *were so excited to see us again that they could hardly contain themselves* (Looper, 2008: 101). This could well be true, and as noted, there is some evidence of real affection between missionary families and their servants in some cases, but one always wonders what it really felt like from the perspective of the servants, especially in view of the inherent imbalances in the employer–servant relationship. Further, the servants were highly unlikely to be able to tell their story, at the time or later, in any kind of public way, in contrast to the missionaries and their children's being able to speak and write about their own perspectives more widely and even internationally.

The servants that the MKs were generally closest to were their nannies (called by various names depending on the country; in India they were called ayahs). As Vallgårda (2015: 192) points out about both most Danish and British missionary families, and as was true about most North American missionary families as well, 'missionary children were allowed to enter into much more intimate relations with native nannies than most adults did with Indians'. The children were often basically raised by their nannies, even breastfed by them in some cases. However, Vallgårda (2015: 192) reminds us, '[t]his is not to say, of course, that missionary parents were not anxious to teach their children to be white, middle class, and properly Christian'. To be sure to establish these differences, and this superiority, missionary children were also dressed differently from, and behaved themselves differently from, local children. Not only was the intention of the missionaries to clearly differentiate their children from local children, but also the parents sought to, in Vallgårda's (2015: 214) telling phrase, 'teach ... [their] children the social categories of empire'. Missionary children were taught that local people were dirty, ignorant, immoral, and untrustworthy. For example, it was assumed that many servants were likely to steal.

My brothers and I had several ayahs during our early childhood years. One, our favorite, was named Peronjini. Although she seemed like an adult to us, she was actually a teenager. We loved her but also were sometimes naughty and disobedient, and sometimes teased her. I wonder now if we would have been as naughty if she hadn't been Indian; did we somehow absorb the idea that white missionaries were 'superior', and that because of her 'inferior' status, we didn't have to obey her?

Some memoirists write about their particularly close relationships with their ayahs or amahs. Noyes (1989), for example, stated that he and his siblings loved their ayah even more than they loved their mother, and that when his family left China, he wanted to stay there with their ayah, Ah Quei. However, Schroth (2011: 21) baldly states what many obviously felt, whether recognizing and acknowledging these feelings or not: *The relationship between an* ayah *and her charge is complicated. While she is the boss, she also isn't. I am a* memsahib, *so I am above her in class. An outcaste, she is from the lowest of the low.* It is significant that Schroth has absorbed the idea of social stratification from learning about and observing the caste system around her in India, and now chooses to use caste as a signifier for social class layers and boundaries that she sees in her relationship with her servant caretaker.

Memoirists writing about their caregivers are often oblivious to the sacrifices those nannies and ayahs had to make. Orr writes of her family's servant Abike, who had a baby:

I don't remember ever seeing her baby though she continued to be my nursemaid. No doubt her mother cared for the new grandchild. I wonder why it was that Abike did not, at least on occasion, bring her child to play with me. I am sorry I missed the opportunities. Because as I look back, I want the Nigerian sisters and brothers I was not allowed to have. (Orr, 2003: 27)

At least two things strike me about this statement. First, Orr is, even writing as an adult, apparently unaware of how so many servants (of missionaries, but also throughout history in many places) had to give up so much of their own family life, including caregiving of their own children, in order to care for the white families' children. In 'wondering' why Abike did not bring her own child to play with her small MK charge, Orr seems unaware of any questions of agency, of whether Abike would be allowed by her employers to bring her own child to work, and of whether she would dare even ask to do so. Orr also makes the whole issue about herself, and about her own perceived loss of 'opportunities', rather than understanding the sacrifices her nursemaid was making.

Orr does show some reflection and an adult awareness of all that she did not know or understand when she was growing up in Nigeria. *As I write this memoir, these hidden moments of a history I thought was mine come to light, and I begin to see that much of what I took for granted was being fought for by someone else* (Orr, 2003: 29). Again, there is much to unpack in this short passage. Her story does reflect that of many MKs, in that MKs often live in a sort of bubble; although they live in a country other than their own, they usually live within carefully defined and maintained physical and social boundaries. She also echoes some of the other memoirists in thinking of the histories of the countries where they were growing up as 'their' histories ('these hidden moments of a history I thought was mine'). She was a child, and this is her memoir, and she is trying to be honest about her feelings; still, there is an unnerving obliviousness and self-centeredness on display here.

This complex relationship, and this attitude of superiority, continued for those of the MKs who went to boarding school. At the schools, there were cooks, servers, cleaners, guards and other local personnel. There was sometimes affection among these personnel and the students, but mostly they were invisible to the MKs. When they were noticed, there was too frequently an attitude of condescension. Lockerbie (1975: 47) writes about boarding school students' 'haughty and disparaging treatment' of the native waiters and kitchen staff. Even the esteemed Gurkhas who served as guards at my boarding school in India, and by whom we students were initially awestruck with admiration, mainly faded into the local scenery and were not regarded as individuals by the missionary children boarders.

Servants were also often (usually but not always gently, even affectionately) mocked by MKs and their parents (similar to O'Neill's expats in Dubai, mentioned above) in what the MKs perceived as 'all in good fun', but in ways that must have felt demeaning to the servants. Schroeder (2013: 64) writes of the time that she told their cook, Tesfai, what to do, coming across as an imperious child commanding an adult. *I hollered, 'Tesfai, I told you a million times – move over!' He and Mom both laughed until tears were pouring down their ... cheeks.* This could possibly be interpreted as charmingly cute behavior, and obviously Schroeder assumes it was interpreted that way not only by her mother but also by the cook, but it seems equally or even more possible that the cook would quietly resent being ordered around by a spoiled little white child. There is no acknowledgement in the memoirist's storytelling of the privilege, insensitivity and rudeness on display in this anecdote.

There is the occasional laughing referral to the perceived ineptness of some servants, even though, if such ineptness were displayed, it was usually because of different cultural and social experiences and knowledge. Orr states with humorous exaggeration that *[o]ne of the great trials of missionary women was to teach Nigerian house servants, always male, to handle the family dishware* (Orr, 2003: 74). Lloret (2004) tells 'funny' stories about maids' behaviors, such as when one ironed a wet diaper dry, or couldn't figure out how a toaster worked, or used far too much starch in the laundry. His tone is humorous, even affectionate and appreciative, but condescending, portraying the servants as ignorant and childish. In the same affectionate but laughing tone, Coleman (2003: 53) writes about how their servant used 'our best lace tablecloth' to carry the wet laundry. He writes about his mother's report of the episode, regarding the servant: 'She said the old thing [the lace tablecloth] was all full of holes, anyway,' cried my laughing mother, while she dabbed her eyes with a hanky. Denton (2003: 80) recounts the 'humorous' story of the 'Chinese helper' *standing and ironing in front of an open refrigerator. It had been too hot so she decided to do something innovative to 'cool down'*. Frerichs (2010) also writes of a favorite story in her family, that of a 'certain native boy' who when told to cook a small pig and put a lemon in the pig's mouth and some parsley behind the pig's ears, came in and served it with the parsley behind his own ears and the lemon in his own mouth.

Sometimes this slight mocking turned into pranks played on servants. Terry, for example, writes rather gleefully as follows:

I pictured the sweltering day when the cook had taken off his shirt and stretched out on his cot to take a nap by the back gate. The temptation was irresistible: I dared Dicky to drop some ice cubes on his bare chest, but he wouldn't take the dare. So I did! Our poor cook couldn't afford to quit his job – and sure put up with a lot of shenanigans! (Terry, 2011: 118)

The sense of unconscious privilege displayed here is breathtaking on so many levels. The cook was probably taking a needed rest, time off from his duties, but apparently had nowhere to rest privately. That the dignity of an adult in this position could be so easily attacked by a heedless and privileged child is certainly disturbing. Terry's cavalier remarks, even writing as an adult, that 'our poor cook couldn't afford to quit his job' emphasize the dependent position of the servant, who has to put up with such indignities from a child in order to keep his job. Her use of the word 'shenanigans' to characterize this and (apparently) other such pranks minimizes and makes light of her attitude and of the behaviors the servant had to accept as a condition of his job.

A few of the memoirists are cognizant that some people criticize missionaries for having servants, and address this criticism head on, a little defensively. Looper, attempting to justify the need for servants, says

> *If a pioneer missionary, such as my parents, is to be able to do any of the work of evangelizing and teaching, they must have help. In a country with no modern amenities, if they do not hire 'houseboys,' cooks, gardeners, and guards to help with the physical labors of living, there would be very little time for family or strength left to devote to evangelizing ... Also, by hiring their services, the missionaries blessed the people who worked for them as there was very little employment available in that country.* (Looper, 2008: 93)

My own parents, fellow missionaries and MKs, and I myself have also felt and expressed such defensive statements, so I cannot quibble with Looper's words, except that I feel a little uncomfortable with the whole rationale, and in particular with the word 'blessed' in this situation, as it seems to glorify the employer–employee relationship unnecessarily, and adds a sort of inappropriately lofty religious tone to the statement.

A small handful of the memoirists are more thoughtful and reflective than most about the situation of having servants. Addleton writes that

> *[t]he notion of 'servants' was always an uncomfortable one, though children for a time could at least maintain the fiction that it did not really matter, that we were instead members of the same family, each with our own assigned roles, feelings, and peculiarities. But the basic inequalities in the relationship were inescapable.* (Addleton, 1997: 27–28)

Alter (1998: 164–165) also questions the implications of having servants: *I had grown up with servants all my life and it was something that I took for granted, even though I sometimes wondered about the roles we played.* He notes that his relationships with the children of the family servants were also fraught. As he grew older, into the high school years, *our friendships became more complicated and slowly we moved apart, as I became aware of the invisible boundaries that lay between us* (Alter, 1998: 164).

Coleman (2003) had a realization even as a child that the practice of having servants embodied the difference between the missionary kids and the local people. He writes with insight and self-awareness about the servants who did the laundry of the MK boarding school students.

> *Every day they ironed the crisp collars and razor-edged creases that set me and my schoolmates apart from the shapeless garments worn by the Ethiopian kids outside the grounds ... My clothes were not just a meeting point, but also a dividing line between them and me. I was from rich, pink people, who paid poor, brown people to clean our clothing. I felt lucky to be on my side of the line.* (Coleman, 2003: 53)

Henderson-James has an interesting perspective on having servants, as she looks back on her time in Angola and compares it with her unease about having a housecleaner in the present in the US.

> *In America ... I had to convince myself that hiring a cleaner was OK. But in Angola, not to have servants would have been remarkable. Wealthy and not so wealthy whites were expected to give employment to the Angolans, and running a large household without help, when all food had to be prepared from scratch and clothes had to be washed by hand would have been hard. In the end, I realized the cleaner and I could have a straightforward exchange of money for service without the paternalism that pervaded the transaction in Angola.* (Henderson-James, 2009: 70)

To circle back to the beginning of this chapter, there was no denying that there was often a close relationship between missionary families and local people, especially servants. As mentioned earlier, there was often genuine affection and loyalty on both sides. When Littell's family left China, there was anguish on the part of both the family and the servants, anguish that seems to have been genuine. He summarizes these feelings by saying *We Littells had always been their 'family'. Leave them behind? Unthinkable!* (Littell, 1995: 34). The part about the 'family' may well be, as discussed above, the missionary families' self-deception, but this statement, although perhaps overly dramatic and self-serving, does recognize that there was a close relationship. Although this is not stated directly, it also recognizes that the servants depended on the missionaries for their jobs and livelihoods.

And yet ... and yet ... as I write this academic, postcolonial-inflected analysis of the relationship of MKs with local people, especially servants, my own memories of our family's servants flood my mind. I remember genuine affection; was I deluded? I will end with a personal story. When, some 30 years after my family left India, one of my brothers took his wife and three children to India so that they could see where he grew up, they visited the town where we had lived the longest. They saw several people that my brother knew back then: church people, staff from the hospital where my physician father worked, friends and servants. Our former gardener, then an old man with a failing memory, saw my brother's family walking toward him, and with great emotion and obvious affection called out to my niece, who was about the same age as I was when I left India, 'It's *Stephanie*! It's *Stephanie*!' When my brother told me this story, I was overwhelmed with emotion myself. I know this story is nostalgic and sentimental, and by feeling that both Srini's and my emotions were genuine, I am contradicting much of what I have said above. Which is real? The emotion or the analysis? Or could they both be real? I tell this story in order to interrogate both the feelings and the academic interpretations, and to remind myself how complex and multilayered the MK experience was for all involved.

5 Schooling

Because the memoirs in this study mainly describe the writers' childhood years, schooling is a big part of their stories. Although the memoirs often describe those experiences as happy ones, unfortunately they also reveal that those experiences were often difficult and sad. For a long time, MK experiences of schooling were not the subject of any kind of sustained, careful study or research. Lockerbie, an educator at Christian schools who undertook research on Christian schools in Asia and Africa, stated that (at the time of writing) the 'education of missionary dependents continues to be the neglected dimension of world mission' (Lockerbie, 1975: viii), and this continues to be somewhat, although less, true to this day.

History

As with the families of British and other European colonial powers in lands far from home, missionary families had to make provision for the schooling of their children. They often followed the traditions established by the colonial families, yet another link between colonial and religious personnel and their traditions and values. In this brief history section, I focus on the example of the British, and later of the North American missionaries, in the country of India, but much of what I say regarding schooling applies to MK schooling in other colonized countries as well.

The similarities between the schooling dilemmas and decisions of British and European colonial families involved in government and trade, on the one hand, and British missionary families, on the other hand, are striking. A detailed example of these connections is given by Brendon in her book, *Children of the Raj* (2005), on children from various backgrounds in India, but especially on British children during the rule of the British. Brendon explains that, until at least the late 19th century, it was more or less assumed that British children would be left in, or sent back to, England for boarding school. However, in the early 20th century there were an increasing number of schools set up in India itself for these English children. In fact, in some cases the schools were set up by missionaries.

There was a social class element to the process of setting these schools up. First, schools were established for the lower classes, such as the children of ordinary soldiers. Gradually schools for the upper classes were built as well. A pattern evolved: the more affluent children attended boarding schools, often in the hill stations; and children of less well-off families attended day schools. Children in boarding schools, despite still being in the same country as their parents, were still separated from them for as much as nine months at a time. It was assumed that these children, coming from the upper classes, were strong and resilient enough to handle the separation, just as those who were left in English boarding schools had been assumed to be able to handle such separation (Brendon, 2005).

Buettner (2004) too, in her book *Empire Families*, writes of the families of the British Raj, and again there is mention of missionary families and schooling; again, we can see the similarities between the schooling issues of the British colonials and those of the missionaries. Buettner (2004: 2) points out 'the integral role of family practices in the reproduction of imperial rule and its personnel', and a large proportion of the family practices that she examines have to do with schooling. Besides the social class element alluded to by Brendon, there was a gender element, discussed by Buettner; families that could not afford to send both boys and girls to school would send just boys. Buettner describes how the British colonials during the later days of the Raj set up schools for children of missionaries in England, and later, as Brendon stated as well, they set up some of the schools for the children of colonials and missionaries.

Foss (2001), the son of a British officer in the Indian Army, tells of attending, just post-World War II, in the hill town of Coonoor in the Nilgiri Hills, 'a boarding school in the hills for the children of the Raj, a small enclave of white boyish faces that studiously followed the pattern and ethos of the British "prep" school' (Foss, 2001: 156). This was very close to the end of the Raj, and there was already a sense at the school of 'a tailing down, approaching a rick in the smooth flow of England's destiny' (Foss, 2001: 159). However, some British schools continued well after the end of the Raj; I myself attended one of them for a few weeks as a day student in kindergarten in a hill station, Ootacumund (popularly known by the British as 'Ooty'), also in the Nilgiri Hills.

There was definitely racism involved, as in India at least, the better British schools in particular were set aside for white Europeans only, meaning that even Anglo-Indians, also known as Eurasians, were often not welcome. Brendon quotes one of her sources as follows: 'No school ... can be expected to impart the character of the pure European to the sons of Madras ayas, Goanese women, or indeed of any native woman, whatever the father may have been' (Brendon, 2005: 135). This statement seems to encapsulate the race and social class distinctions that were so important to the British residents of the British empire. When new schools were set up during World War II, because children could not travel to England or elsewhere during war time, or their parents feared to let them do so, these schools were often even more restrictive, admitting only the children of wealthier families. One measure of how desirable these schools were for some parents was a snobbish one: they did not want their children to develop the 'dreaded chi chi accent' found among lower class and/or Eurasian children (Brendan, 2005: 138).

Simultaneously with the building of British schools in India was the building of a few American schools; one of the earliest was Woodstock School in Mussoorie, founded in 1854; some of the memoirists in this study (Alter, Brush, Schoonmaker) attended Woodstock. These schools were generally well regarded, but less snobbish, exclusive and racist than the most prominent British schools. Some of them accepted a few Anglo-Indian and Indian children, and some of Brendan's informants speak of close interracial friendships.

Soon American missionary boards and groups opened other boarding schools for missionaries' children in several countries; the one I attended from ages 10 to 15 was Kodaikanal ('Kodai') School (founded in 1901), in the Palni Hills of India. The schools served American children and a scattering of other Western children, with a very few children from the countries in which they were located; this changed over the years, and now, for example, Kodaikanal School is billed as a Christian international school but the majority of its students are Indian and often not Christian. By the way, guessing that some readers might have an image of boarding schools as being 'posh' and expensive, I note that these boarding schools were generally functional and reasonably comfortable but far from luxurious. Heating, hot water and consistent electricity, for example, were unreliable.

There was of course some flexibility about schooling for MKs. Each missionary family, in each circumstance, had to make up its own plan regarding schooling, although often bound by mission board policies, funding options (usually mission boards paid for MKs' schooling) and of course the availability and locations of appropriate schools. Post-war, most MKs went to missionary schools, or occasionally 'international' schools, most often boarding schools. In later years, after the 1970s, some were homeschooled, especially very young children. There was considerable overlap among these three possibilities (day schools, boarding schools and homeschooling) throughout these eras. What did not happen, except in very rare cases, was MKs attending local schools for local children. One exception was Espey (1994), whose parents (missionaries in China) sent him and his sister to a local Chinese kindergarten for a year, mostly to improve their Chinese language skills. However, after that year, Espey and his sister went on to English-language schools in China. The local schools for local children were not considered good enough for the MKs. In addition, it was considered that MKs had to be educated in the American system so they could fit back in, and be prepared, when they returned to North America. No one, parents or children, seemed to challenge this belief as being paramount. However, at least one memoirist noted the irony of a Western education in non-Western countries: Orr writes dryly that *[i]t seemed perfectly reasonable to learn European history while living on the edges of the Nigerian rain forest* (Orr, 2003: 108). Unfortunately, although there is quite a bit of academic literature about international schools (e.g. Grimshaw & Sears, 2008; Hayden, 2006; Langford, 2001; Okada, 2009), there is far less research specifically on missionary-based schools. One exception is Dow's book (2003), which discusses the Rift Valley Academy in Kenya; the author puts the history of the school in the context of the history of Kenya itself and the growth of Christianity there. Another is by Seaman (1997), about the Murree Christian School in Pakistan.

Missionary Schools for Local Children

Meanwhile, running alongside these developments in the education of the children of colonials and missionaries was the missionaries' efforts to educate local children. Such children were very, very rarely allowed to attend the same schools as white colonial and missionary children. However, missionaries did start and maintain a number and variety of schools and orphanages for local children. In Vallgårda's 2015 study of Danish missionary schools and orphanages in South India in the late 19th and early 20th centuries, she describes these schools, as well as the missionaries' well-intentioned but condescending and, in effect, racist attitudes. She states that '[t]hese evangelicals increasingly came to see themselves as the loving saviors of the poor heathen children' (Vallgårda, 2015: 2). She further says that the Danish missionaries in India as well as in other countries, like other European and North American missionaries, reflected the views of their fellow citizens back home in considering their work with children as 'a project of *white adults saving brown children from brown adults*' (p. 3; emphasis in original), adding that this is 'an image that persists in present-day humanitarian discourses about children in the Global South' (Vallgårda, 2015: 3). These missionaries were so sure that their ways of raising and educating children were modern and superior that they even felt justified in sometimes removing children from their parents, either putting them in orphanages or boarding schools or in some case fostering the children themselves (Vallgårda, 2015).

Boarding Schools

Since the bulk of the MK memoirists I studied went to boarding schools, I focus on their experiences in those settings. One of the most difficult aspects of boarding schools was that some MKs started in these schools as young as four or five years old. Phemister, for example, was sent away to school at age four, which most people would consider a shockingly young age for a child to be purposely separated from her parents; further, she didn't see her mother again for a year and a half. Jacoby and others started boarding school at age five. Boarding school was hard for many MKs, but particularly difficult for the very young children. Lloret (2004: 26), for one, remembers that *[b]y far the most difficult two years of schooling ... came in our early years. I went away to school for first grade, not just to an MK boarding school, but to Huehue Academy, which was four countries away, in Guatemala*. The schools were 1–3 days' travel away from their homes with their parents, and sometimes in different countries. Many attended several schools; Lloret (2006: 26) *attended ten different schools during the course of my K–12 career* (counting schools back in the US).

Some memoirists loved boarding school, some hated it and some were merely resigned to it. Like it or not, they almost never had a choice. They were taught that their going away to school was part of God's will and would allow their parents to do God's work. As one mother put it, in statements that sound harsh to most people, missionaries' *time and energy must not be siphoned off for teaching one's children at home*, and *the ache of leaving children in the care of others was ... just one of the many sacrifices she had promised the Lord that she was willing to make in His service* (Phemister, 2009: 70). Children were told *God first, others second, and ourselves last of all*, so they learned to live with the fact that *we were always saying goodbye* (Addleton, 1997: 64). Or as Harvey (2009: 15), who started boarding school at age five, thousands of miles from her family, poignantly puts it, *Child self says: 'Now we can't have Mommy and Daddy. They have to stay at home to tell African families and their children about Jesus'*. She later goes on to say, *One of the lessons I learned ... was that Christ considered MK children less important than Africa children* (p. 110). It is sad that some MKs were absorbing this message that both Jesus and their own parents considered them a lower priority than their religion and other children, and on top of that, felt they could not complain in any way.

The unhappiest memoirists, either from homesickness or, in the worst cases, from experiencing abuse (more on this below), were generally those in very strict schools run by very conservative missions. Jacoby (2011: 153) says that she *was spared the kinds of corrosive experiences some mish kids have had as a result of a too-rigid conservative outlook*, thereby referencing the common belief (which is supported by some of the memoirs in this study) that the conservative religious schools were the most destructive and traumatic for children.

Missionary children and teenagers experienced an unusual mixture of privilege and non-privilege. They had much colonial privilege as white children (all the memoirists were white, although of course there were a few, very few, North American missionaries of other races in some countries). They were also relatively well-off materially compared with the local people. Furthermore, they knew that they would (with extremely rare exceptions) be heading back to North America eventually. Finally, they gained status and privilege from the fact that their parents were in positions of authority in the churches, hospitals, schools and communities where they worked. (The topic of MK social class privilege is further discussed in Chapter 8.) However, these areas of privilege were diluted by other aspects of the MKs' situations. As children, MKs had even less control over their lives than many other children do. They were under the control of their parents, Mission Boards and – they were taught – God. All children are largely controlled by their parents, but in these cases there were added layers of authority from Mission Boards, churches, boarding school administrators and teachers, and religious beliefs. The parents believed in their own work, and in the importance of sharing their religion, and thus were part of the colonial enterprise; they wittingly or unwittingly also involved their children in the practices of religious colonialism, and in addition, in the unintended consequences of that strand of colonialism. The children often felt helpless, caught up in a situation over which they had no control, and then felt guilty for resenting the situation. Many MKs enjoyed their schooling and had positive experiences, but the consequences of colonialism and the constraints of missionary life often caused problems, and can be seen more specifically in some of the issues the MKs encountered and wrote about, the most difficult of which I now discuss below.

Feelings of homesickness, unhappiness, abandonment and grief

Especially for the children who started boarding school as young as four, five, six or seven years old, it was unfathomable that their parents would leave them with strangers for months at a time. Even some older children dreaded going to, or going back to after vacations at home, boarding school. Van Valkenburg (2014: 9) says, *There are absolutely no words to describe the horrifying feelings of grief as the day to leave for boarding school approached.* Schroeder (2013: 127) not only felt grief but also, *anger washed over me.* Schroth (2011: 77) delineates the constant comings and goings of her siblings in boarding school, and when she attended such a school herself, she bursts out *I hate boarding school!* Bascom (2006: 93), when he was dropped off at boarding school at age seven, *felt as if I had tipped off a cliff and begun a long, long fall.* Orr (2003: 173) writes that she *found herself in boarding school, or rather I lost myself.* Alter (1995: 118) says that when his parents first left, he *felt abandoned and alone* and afterward he *often felt the pangs of homesickness* (p. 132). Bascom (2006: 6) remembers watching his older brother as he was left behind at boarding school for the first time: *[W]e simply left Johnathan there, standing next to his new dorm mother ... Johnathan's face crumpled as we drove away.* Henderson-James (2009: 51) speaks of being away from her family as a *fog of longing and loss ... Homesickness sat in my stomach like a ball of lead ... I was lonely.* Bascom (2006: 109) writes that, one day, *suddenly, against my will, I became aware of myself as a solitary entity ... I felt a strange emptiness.* Later he writes, *My old feeling of being lost crept back as I lay in the dark – as if no one knew where I was, not even me* (p. 203). Peters (1996: 26) tries but fails to be matter-of-fact about boarding schools, describing them as *schools for missionary kids who were abandoned so that their parents could serve the Lord somewhere else.* The belief revealed by this last quotation is echoed by some other memoirists, who were told or who intuited that their parents' missionary work ('God's work') had to come first. As Coleman (2003: 69) put it, *God came first, family second. We children were loved, but we stood in line behind God.*

Unfortunately, the people put in charge of boarding school children, such as the house parents, were often not helpful. Many of them had no special training in education or child psychology, and sometimes they were staff members who had failed at other missionary work. Skarsten remembers all the homesick and lonely children, including herself, at boarding school, and says that coping with these feelings would have been a lot easier if I could have responded as a child, expressing my feelings of fear, loneliness and sadness, if someone could have been there to comfort and reassure me. I cannot recall ever once getting a hug or any physical demonstration of affection from a dorm parent. Nor do I recall intervention or protection against some of the cruelties that went on in the dorms and playgrounds. (Skarsten, 1992: 29)

Skarsten also points out that MKs in boarding school could not express feelings of inadequacy or sadness, because they are 'all trained from an early age to have an exterior of self-assurance, strength and independence. No show of weakness was ever permitted. In this we felt a semblance of control, in a situation which rendered us otherwise powerless' (Skarsten, 1992: 29).

Of course it was very hard for the parents, too, to leave their children in boarding school, so far away, to see them only (usually) twice a year for vacations, and to be able to contact them only through weekly letters. The events in these memoirs took place long before email and Facetime existed, and even long-distance telephone calls were very expensive and rare. Bascom's mother, for example, often cried when she had to say goodbye to her children when they left for boarding school, and was heard to say repeatedly, *He's too young* (Bascom, 2006: 7). Schmitthenner's wife Ruth, when these two MKs grew up and became missionaries themselves, said that *being separated from the children is the hardest part of missionary life* (Schmitthenner, 2004: 117). However, the facts are that the parents were adults, not children, and that they had chosen the situation, as their children had not. I do not want to sound unsympathetic; I truly do sympathize with the parents; as a parent myself, I cannot imagine having a child or children so far away at such a young age, with so little opportunity to communicate. Still, there is no comparison between the parents' situation and that of their children, the MKs.

Not all children felt abandoned and unhappy when they attended boarding school. Some were of course sad to be away from their families, but were fortunate enough to enjoy the adventures and friendships they experienced in their schools. Reimer, for example, who seems relentlessly positive about most things, at least as shown in her memoir, states that she loved grade school in Swaziland, didn't have trouble adjusting when she was back in the US for a furlough, and *really enjoyed* high school (Reimer, 1975: 42). Other memoirists describe their school experiences in a very matter-of-fact way, often emphasizing the enjoyable and unusual experiences they had. Some say that they missed their families, and at the same time felt unconnected from local people, so finally had to depend on each other, their fellow students. Addleton (1998: 71) describes this process as *fall[ing] back on each other, creating our own micro-universe*, a statement that rings true for me, remembering my own boarding school days (but I was fortunate in that the situation didn't make me feel sad). Still others just give the bare facts of where they were schooled, and say little or nothing about their feelings. Coleman has a somewhat unusual view of the boarding school experience: since his family moved around within Ethiopia, his boarding school was actually *where I grew up* and *the constant* in his life (Coleman, 2003: 26) and he *loved school* (p. 66). However, I must say, and this was a surprise to me, as someone who mostly enjoyed boarding school: the predominance of the memoirists who went to boarding schools experienced, and wrote about, severe pain, sadness, homesickness and feelings of abandonment.

Feelings of resignation or rebellion

The main way in which many of the MKs in boarding schools coped was with a sort of resignation. They knew they had no choice, and it was useless to protest. Schroeder (2013: 127) writes that *I wanted to be back home in Bobeecho, not going to boarding school. Anger washed over me*, but then asks herself *What use was it to think this way. I couldn't change anything by being upset*. Most of them learned to follow the rules, to lie low and not attract attention. A smaller number took the opposite tack and rebelled, acted out and broke as many rules as possible. Sometimes they took out their unhappiness on fellow students, hazing or bullying them. Perhaps these rebellious students hoped to get ejected from the school, but mostly they just got punished, or were transferred to other schools.

Stresses on family life and family relationships

It is not surprising that MKs in boarding schools not only missed their families, but sometimes felt very separate from, and even alienated from, their parents. Often they felt close to siblings who were undergoing the same experiences, but sometimes they could not even find comfort in, or provide comfort to, each other. Orr feels that going to boarding school *result[ed] in a kind of basic separation from what should be closest to you: your country and your mother* (Orr, 2003: 99). Vividly, she also feels that

> *[b]oarding school was like swimming underwater and only underwater. You couldn't come up for air. And after a while you adjusted to this world where relationships are distorted and you can't judge distance. You actually forget how it feels to breathe.* (Orr, 2003: 183–184)

Abuse

The most horrific aspect of life in boarding school for a small but significant number of MKs was physical, sexual and emotional abuse. In some cases, there was bullying and hazing by students of each other. Orr says there was *sexual hazing* and *ritualized beatings* by students at her school (Orr, 2003: 277). Friesen too writes of bullying by other kids. Even more horrifying was abuse, sometimes systematic, by school staff members. Harvey (2009: 21) writes a particularly blistering and heartbreaking portrayal of abuse at her school, the (later notorious) Mamou Academy in New Guinea. She tells of children's often being threatened, *savagely beaten* and humiliated. She further writes that cruel teachers forced some children to sit in their own urine and feces for hours. Children often screamed for help for hours and were ignored. She and other students were sexually abused, including fondling, oral sex and sodomy. She was raped by her housefather. Seaman too was abused by two teachers. The students were told not to tell anyone, and because they felt (understandably) helpless and scared, they didn't.

In some schools, abuse of students went on for decades, and the children affected were helpless to do anything while at the school. They were not able to talk to anyone about the abuse. Their parents were far away, and their letters were read by school administrators before they were mailed. Other adults at the school, not personally implicated in the abuse, were either incapable of believing, or unwilling to believe in, wrongdoing by the fellow missionaries who were administrators, teachers, support staff and house parents. Even when children were home with their parents for the holidays, they often did not tell them about the abuse, thinking they would not be believed, or that somehow the perpetrators would punish them and their families. Parents unwittingly exacerbated the situation by encouraging their children to be compliant and obedient, both at home and in boarding school (Zylstra, 2014). Some children were told by their abusers that if they told anyone about the abuse, their parents would no longer be able to do God's work on the mission field (Zylstra, 2014). Because of this, and because of other threats, some students not only suffered but also felt abandoned by other adults and by God. Harvey (2009: 125) says, *In my experience, God and the abusive houseparents merged into one.*

These experiences of abuse left scars on the abused MKs for a long time, sometimes their whole lives. Walters (2007), who has counseled many MKs, points out that abuse by those who are supposed to be spiritual leaders (missionaries, teachers and house parents at missionary schools, etc.) has particularly shaming and confusing results; if a person who is supposed to be doing God's work, and whom one is supposed to look up to and obey, can do these terrible things, what does that mean for one's belief in God and religion? Walters (2007: 287) calls this 'spiritual abuse'. She offers some hope by noting that the MKs who were able to tell someone, and especially those who received counseling, found that they were able, at least to some extent, to heal and move past the terrible memories.

It was only years later, when MK alumni of these schools started talking with each other, that the abuse was exposed. The most famous example of a school with widespread abuse that was finally discovered was the Christian and Missionary Alliance's Mamou Academy in Guinea, West Africa. From 1950 to 1971, children were 'beaten with belts, forced to eat their own vomit, punched and slapped in the face, coerced into performing oral sex, required to sit in their own feces, fondled, and beaten with a strap to the point of bleeding' (Kennedy, 1998: n.p.). After alumni spoke of their experiences, there was an investigation leading to the Mamou Academy report of 1995. One of the children who was abused at Mamou was Harvey (mentioned above); another was the memoirist Paul Friesen (also mentioned above), who from the age of six experienced terribly excessive and inappropriate discipline and humiliation, as well as bullying by other children. He has experienced intense distress and depression ever since, and his memoir is one long cry of pain. Also discovered to have been the sites of serious abuse were several boarding schools run by the New Tribes Mission in Senegal, where at least 50 MKs were abused in the late 1980s (Zylstra, 2010).

Most boarding schools did not have instances of abuse of their students, or at least none were mentioned in the memoirs and other sources, and even in the ones that did, not all faculty and staff participated. However, some who did not participate are guilty of turning their heads the other way and not acknowledging or speaking out about what was happening. Since these instances of abuse came to light, some changes have been made, but there have also been 'denominational denial, revictimization, and partial apology', and some mission agencies are still in denial, or are too slow or too half-hearted in changing their policies and actions (Harvey, 2009: 198). However, fortunately, many mission board policies have become much stricter and more careful, with background checks and training of administrators, teachers and staff required. Other factors improving the situation include the 2003 US federal law making it a crime for Americans to have sex with minors overseas, and the fact that insurance companies will not insure schools for abuse if they do not have appropriate policies in place. Another important factor is that there are now fewer mission boarding schools around the world. Zylstra (2014) states that, according to the Association of Christian Schools International, there are currently about 150 schools serving missionary kids, but only 30 of these offer boarding. It is heartening that matters have improved, but we can never forget these terrible incidents of abuse, and all involved organizations and personnel – church leaders, school administration and parents – need to be vigilant. We need to remember these terribly exploited children. It must have taken great courage for abused students to speak up, even years later, and/or to write about the abuse in their memoirs and elsewhere. By doing so, they have helped to expose the abuse, bring some abusers to justice, change school policies and practices, and lessen the level of abuse in recent years. Nevertheless, it is horrible to think that any instances at all have existed in the past and may still be occurring.

Re-entry into North American life

Whether MKs had good or bad experiences in the countries where their parents worked, and in their schools, they almost universally experienced cultural shock and adjustments when they returned to North America, whether for furloughs of a year or two, or permanently. As with all of the experiences and feelings described in the memoirs, there is a wide variety of responses to 're-entry', from minor periods of adjustment, such as Alter's (1998: 59) statement that *[t]here were so many things we didn't understand*, to intensely difficult and long-lasting problems. Alter also describes the ordeal that many missionary families had to undergo 'back home' of going to different churches to speak about their missionary work and to solicit funding. He says, *I was the mish-kid from India, exhibited like a freak of nature* (Alter, 1998: 71).

Note that although I have (above) divided the memoirists' schooling experiences into several issues, these issues often intersect and interact, and often have repercussions well into the MKs' futures. For instance, MKs who felt abandoned at boarding schools by their parents were obviously relieved to live at home again, but sometimes it was too late to ameliorate the negative feelings, or the 'closing down' in self-protection, brought about by being so far from their families for such big portions of the years. Children who were abused were clearly profoundly relieved not to be in their schools any more, but the residual effects of the abuse often lasted a lifetime. As with the broader category of Third Culture Kids (Gregory, 2002), MKs often found living with their families again, and living back in North America again, more difficult experiences than they or others might have expected.

One of many vivid descriptions of sad and upsetting feelings upon returning to the US is that of Bascom. When he was nine years old, his family returned to the US for a furlough. At first he felt strong, as if the fact that he had survived boarding school meant he could survive anything. However, after he realized he had left his special windbreaker on a ferry, he collapsed. As for many children and even adults, sometimes one symbolic event is the proverbial straw that breaks the camel's back. He angrily and sadly asks himself, *Who was I anyway, this half-African, half-American creature, this missionary Gypsy brought to America?* and goes on to say, *I cried until I couldn't cry anymore, and when I fell asleep, I slept like the dead, not waking until midday. I felt very small in the noonday light* (Bascom, 2006: 225). He later reflects that when he was in boarding school as a child in Ethiopia, he had actually been removed from Ethiopian culture, *cordoned off in a fenced school in Addis Ababa* (Bascom, 2006: 234). Another such wrenching description of the pain of leaving the mission field was Orr's: *All the relations of my early life were ripped from me like hair by the roots* (Orr, 2003: 295).

Re-entry was often especially difficult for MKs in the middle school and high school years. Lloret remembers this time as follows:

> *I was thrown into a suburban Dallas junior high school and felt like I had moved to another world ... quite a shock to my eighth grade psyche ... All I wanted was to be like all the other kids, and yet I knew I was different because of my experiences overseas. I even felt a bit embarrassed trying to explain where I was from as no one, it seemed, had ever heard of Costa Rica.* (Lloret, 2004: 36)

The re-entry difficulties were exacerbated by the common difficulties of any child or teenager entering a new school, having to figure out the culture and customs of that school, hoping to make new friends, but often being ignored, shunned or bullied for being 'different'. They soon learned not to talk much about their MK backgrounds and travels, as North American kids were not very interested, and often thought such backgrounds just made the MKs weird. Alter, for example, went to school in the US for sixth grade, and found that

> *fitting into junior high required more than just boasting about my experiences in Landour [the site of his school in India]. There was a whole new culture that I had to assimilate and comprehend as quickly as I could. If I wanted to become an American I had to act and sound like one of them. Most of sixth grade was a struggle to be accepted, to blend into the tumult of an American adolescence.* (Alter, 1998: 147)

Also an issue is the paradoxical fact that many MKs were quite sheltered in the countries outside the US where they lived. Despite being experienced in travel and knowledge of other cultures, they often were restricted by their parents' religious beliefs. For example, some had never gone to movies or dances, and had never dated. This became another matter to try to understand, and another way that they needed to try to fit in. Some did not cope well, and got into various types of trouble, such as using drugs or getting pregnant.

In contrast to the examples above, a few of the memoirists were candid, almost vehement, in their celebration of going back to North America. Braaten speaks of his boarding school experiences rather neutrally and briefly, but says he was definitely not sad to leave. He says that he

> *could not wait to get back to America and the benefits of civilization I had been deprived of during my teen years. When I landed on American soil, I felt that I had come home at last – the land of my birth.* (Braaten, 2010: 7)

I myself returned with my family to the US from India at the age of 15, and the transition was, at least at first, not easy. I was upset at having to leave my home, school and friends, and I blamed my parents for the move, even though they had no real choice. Starting again in a new school in a 'new' country at the beginning of my junior year in high school was hard emotionally and socially, although I attended an excellent school and soon adapted. Especially at first, I often felt like an outsider, unfamiliar with the specific customs of American high school life and teenagers, and constantly monitored myself to stave off embarrassing mistakes and misunderstandings that would betray that 'outsider' status. Overall, I was fortunate in that the transition had few lasting effects, but I must admit that, even these decades later, I sometimes feel insecure about knowing what to do in certain social or other situations where the answers come easily to those who grew up in North America.

Several of the memoirists write that the negative aspects of their MK experiences and identities affected them strongly for the rest of their lives. Some never completely recovered from trauma, feelings of abandonment and other damaging events and consequences. Friesen, Harvey and Van Reken in particular write about their lifelong struggles. Littell, who seems to have had a very dysfunctional family, became estranged from his parents for some time in his twenties, and tells of extensive problems in his family, such as psychological issues, illnesses and early deaths, as well as multiple marriages and divorces. He feels that his parents neglected him, and now worries that he has neglected his own daughters, concluding that there are multigenerational effects of MK life.

I do want to reiterate that, despite these problems experienced by many MKs, many loved their boarding schools, and although they missed their parents, they were very happy among their friends in boarding schools. Some, like me, were sad to leave their schools and friends to go 'home' for furloughs or even permanently. Alter, for example, writes that he didn't like being in the US for furlough, and couldn't wait to get back to India and his school there. I myself, although of course I missed my parents, liked boarding school very much. I had (mostly) good teachers, made good friends, learned a lot and had some great experiences and adventures. I never knew anyone who was obviously terribly unhappy in our school, and I never heard of any abuse. This does not mean that it never occurred there, and in retrospect I recall one instance about which there were vague rumors, but I was naïve at the time and couldn't imagine that the rumors could be true. However, I think that in general there was a healthy atmosphere at my school.

My first inkling of some boarding school children feeling unhappy came when I read, some years ago and long before I started this current book project, the memoir of Ruth Van Reken (a memoir that is included in this study), in which she tells how miserable and abandoned she felt during her boarding school years in Nigeria. I was surprised and sad to read of her feelings, but also intrigued, and reminded of how my own experience didn't necessarily coincide with those of other MKs in boarding schools around the world. In some ways, reading Van Reken's memoir was one genesis of this book on MK memoirs.

Interestingly, a surprising number of memoirists never mention their schooling in the countries where their parents worked, or mention it very briefly, almost in passing. I am not sure how to interpret this, since school is such a large proportion of most children's and adolescents' lives. Perhaps for these memoirists, school was just routine and not very important, or they feel that describing it would not be of much interest to readers of their memoirs. Or perhaps they are repressing bad memories. More likely, I imagine, is that their schooling situations were fine, but not memorable to them.

A Mixed Legacy

I am very aware that these problems experienced by many MKs were no worse than those experienced by millions of children around the world, including some immigrant and other minority children who also experience abuse, adjustment problems and psychological problems, and in addition may suffer from poverty, lack of health care and adequate education, and more. It is also absolutely true that MKs' privilege in many areas (e.g. race, social class, colonial history, resources) ameliorates, at least to some extent, some of their difficulties. Still, I feel it is important to understand and acknowledge the experiences of this particular group of young people, without saying that they are more or less deserving of understanding and yes, sympathy, especially for those who experienced the worst of the difficulties. They too were, at times, victims of the colonial enterprise and specifically the missionary enterprise.

6 Learning Local Languages (or Not)

The 'Privilege' of Being a Monolingual English Speaker

English has become an increasingly privileged and valued, perhaps overvalued, language in much of the world. It has long been associated with both British and American colonialism. It is also, in many countries and situations, associated with social class: those of higher social classes often are educated in, and speak, English (as, or in addition to, their first language). Not only is English the language of privilege in so many countries around the world, but it also allows the specific privilege in Western English-dominant countries of not learning other languages, as seen in, for example, the large proportion of residents of the US who are monolingual. The generally accepted figure for Americans who speak only one language is about 80% (Potowski, 2010). Many North Americans do not learn other languages even when they live in other countries.

North American missionaries share this 'privilege' of not needing to learn additional languages, but generally choose to waive it. The missionary parents of the memoirists usually learn, or try to learn, local languages. Not only is this useful in their work, but also it is a sign of commitment to the area where they are working. Nehrbass (2016) points out that people in the countries where missionaries work measure them and their commitment to the country partly based on whether they learn local languages or not. My own parents worked hard and spent many weeks, months and years studying and learning several Indian languages for their work: Telugu, Oriya and Saora, and in my father's case, Tamil as well. I can still remember seeing and hearing my parents sitting on the verandah of our house every day for several hours with their *munshee* (teacher), going over and over the alphabet, the pronunciation, the grammar, the vocabulary. My father was particularly interested in, and gifted at, language learning; he studied Latin and Greek and other languages in college, and years after his missionary service, living in and practicing medicine in California, he studied and learned Spanish. My mother was a French major in college, and also worked hard at learning and became quite fluent in the local languages where we lived.

I want to note that in some cases missionaries learned local languages not only to enable them to do their mission work, whether ministerial, medical or educational, but also to help to preserve local languages, through doing translation work (often of the Bible) (Makoni & Makoni, 2009).

English language learners (such as immigrants, refugees, long-term visitors and international students) in the US, the UK and other English-dominant countries need, or feel they need, English as a form of privilege, or simply to navigate their lives, whether they like it or not. Additionally, many residents of non-English-dominant countries learn English because they perceive that knowing this international language will probably help them to succeed in their careers and lives. Knowing or not knowing English has far-reaching, sometimes unforeseen, effects. For example, Sandhu (2014) describes the way that in India an English language education, as opposed to a vernacular language education, often makes a huge difference in how successful a woman is in her career or in how marriageable she is. This is also a matter of social class status; in many places, it is a distinct asset and a sign of higher social class to know and use the English language fluently and correctly.

Missionary Kids Learning Local Languages – Or Not

Missionary kids have far less need than their parents to learn local languages, and unlike immigrants or international students in other countries, or even strivers in their own countries, do not need to learn other languages. They are thus able to exercise their privilege to be monolingual English speakers. Unlike the other learners just mentioned, North American MKs learned, if they did learn, local languages in the countries of their parents' missionary work based on such factors as convenience or enjoyment, but not because they really needed it. They already possessed the privileged language: English. This is not to say that the MKs were consciously thinking in this way ('I don't need to learn this language so why should I?'), but the result was the same as if they were; this is an example of unconscious privilege.

Despite the 'privilege' of not having to learn local languages, some MKs, including several of the memoirists in this study, do either learn, or attempt to learn, the local languages of the countries in which their parents do mission work. Some learn the languages quickly and well; others struggle or give up. Others do not even try. Some love using the local languages; others do not. For some, it is a way of connecting with the local people and culture; others would, consciously or unconsciously, prefer to keep their 'superior' status by not mingling much with local people. Or they do in fact want to connect with local people, but they don't want it enough to do the hard work of learning their languages.

As I analyzed the 42 book-length MK memoirs in my study, I noted references to the MKs learning (or not learning) local languages. I had in mind the following questions, among others: how many of the MKs attempted to learn local languages? How many succeeded? To what extent? What were their attitudes toward the local languages?

For context, I offer my own story. First, I confess that I am not proud of my history with Indian languages, nor with my attitudes as a child toward them, but they are, I believe, somewhat representative of many (although far from all) other MKs' attitudes and behaviors. When my family first arrived in India, I was very young, and I rather rapidly learned some Telugu, the main language of Andhra Pradesh. At ages 2–4, I was a quick learner, especially as I had an Indian ayah with whom I spent a good portion of the day. I even translated for my parents, who as adults learned more slowly. Then my family moved to another part of India, Orissa, where a different language, Oriya, was spoken. Although my parents, especially my father, learned Oriya for their work, my brothers and I learned very little of that language. We must have known a bit, because our ayah there didn't speak much English, but I have almost no memory of speaking it, whereas I do remember speaking Telugu. When I was about 10 and, after a furlough in Canada and the US, we were back in Andhra Pradesh, my parents wanted my brothers and me to learn Telugu. So we were given lessons by a tutor. However, we were poor students, not really motivated, and would play pranks on the tutor and invent reasons to cancel or shorten our lessons. We knew enough Telugu to get by when needed, but we weren't motivated to learn much more. When I was in boarding school in Madras State (now Tamil Nadu) soon afterwards, the local language was Tamil, and I learned a little by osmosis, but again, never got too far with it. From my perspective now, as an applied linguist and language educator, I think 'What a lost opportunity!' However, the bottom line then was that I, along with my brothers and many other MKs, knew, subconsciously at least, that we didn't really need the Indian languages, and soon enough would be back in North America where those languages would be irrelevant. After leaving India, I gradually forgot all but a few words of the Telugu I knew as a child. In talking with other MKs, and in reading the memoirs of other MKs in various countries, I find that, with some exceptions, their experiences and attitudes were similar to mine. They were not negative about local languages, but were not much motivated to learn them. I am always impressed by MKs who can still, many years later, speak the languages they learned as children but seldom have occasion to use now.

Local languages are much less mentioned in the memoirs in this study than one might imagine in the stories of children who spent many years in different countries, surrounded by multiple languages. Many of the memoirs do not mention learning local languages at all. Either the authors did not learn the languages, or they did not consider languages an important enough topic to include in their memoirs. Several (17) barely mention the topic, with perhaps a sentence or paragraph devoted to it. Only a handful (nine) of these 17 discuss their own learning of languages more than minimally. Some, like my brothers and I, didn't feel any confidence about learning, or just didn't put the effort into it. However, some learned enough of a local language to manage some conversation; Frerichs (2010: 222), for example, says that *none of us learned Kotte or any other language, except for Tok Pisin, the lingua franca [in New Guinea]*.

A few MKs do mention learning local languages very well, sometimes to the point that they did not use English at all, as in the case of Deters, who learned Portuguese in Brazil. She and her sister *were thrown headfirst into Brazilian culture. Not one word of English was spoken in our daily lives, except by our parents ... [we] mastered Portuguese quickly* (Deters, 2009: 71). However, then when she returned to the US after six years in Brazil, she barely spoke English. *I could no longer understand spoken English, let alone read or write English* (p. 167), she says. This is an extreme case among the memoirists in my study, and it caused serious problems for Deters's education back in the US. Other memoirists, such as Looper, were truly bilingual as young children, learning both English and a local language. Looper (2008: 145) says that at age five, *I spoke Moré even more fluently than I did English*. One young boy, Cordell's brother Burt, spent the first two years of his life in India, learned Marathi, and during the family's first furlough in North America, refused to speak English for a while. Alter (1998: 101) also remembers that *[m]y own mother tongue was a mixture of Hindustani and English. For the first five years of my life, I used both languages interchangeably, even with my parents.*

Some memoirists even spoke several languages. In Coleman's (2003: 47) case, he became trilingual: *[W]hen I came in for supper, I related my adventures in three languages: the local mixture of Oromifa and Amharic for Ha-da Saifu, the woman who worked in our home, and a combination of English and Amharic for my mother.* Henderson-James, whose parents worked in Angola, learned Portuguese, English, French and Umbundu. She also loved learning Latin at school, so languages were obviously important and interesting to her. Kuegler, the daughter of linguist missionaries, learned Nepalese, Danuwar Rai, German, Indonesian and Fayu.

Children who had ayahs or amahs (nannies) often learned smatterings of local languages from them, as my brothers and I did from our various ayahs. For example, Noyes (1989: 14) says, *We had learned our first words from her [their amah] and preferred her up-country dialect to our parents' more correct Cantonese.* (Linguists would prefer another word such as 'standard' to the word 'correct' in this sentence.) Others, especially boys, learned from their playmates. For example, Schroeder writes that her brothers learned to speak Amharic because they played with local boys. MK girls were less likely to play with local children. Linguists have long believed that children generally learn second or third languages more quickly than adults do (although currently this view is being challenged by some scholars), so some very young MKs sometimes served as translators for their parents, as I did, especially in the families' early years in the new country. Also, whereas their parents learned written languages, frequently so they could read or sometimes translate documents (often the Bible) into local languages, children often only learned to speak languages but not to read or write them. They usually had even less need to read or write the languages than to speak them. Each MK has a different and specific relationship with local languages, even though most of the memoirists in this study do not discuss the topic at all, or in detail, in their memoirs. Orr (2003: 19) says rather poetically, but perhaps sentimentally and perhaps partaking in discourses of the exotic, *I learned Nigerian accents in my ears if not on my tongue. The languages sound like music.*

Languages and Schooling

Note that the examples above refer to learning by osmosis from ayahs, playmates and other informal sources. Almost none of the memoirists learned local languages through actual lessons at their schools or elsewhere. I believe that my school in India at one point offered a class in Tamil, the language of the area where the school was located, but I don't remember hearing much about it, or knowing of anyone taking the class. In fact, not only did these missionary and international schools teach in English, but the schools and colleges set up by missionaries for local people, originally taught in local languages, often gradually shifted to English as well.

Even children who learned local languages found their learning disrupted when they went to boarding school in another area, or when they went back to North America for furloughs of a year or more, and certainly when they eventually moved home for high school or college. Reimer, for instance, learned Afrikaans in Swaziland, but after a furlough in the US, had forgotten most of it and had to regain it at the bilingual (English and Afrikaans) school she attended for her last two years of high school.

Language-related Attitudes and Antics

Some MKs got into trouble involving language when they learned 'bad' or 'swear' words in a local language, and scandalized both the locals and their own parents. For example, Dilley (2012: 34) remembers that her brother Ben, at the age of five, *learned how to swear in Bukusu, the local tribal language, and one of the neighbors went to his mother to ask if she knew what her son was saying*; the mother, naturally, was appalled and embarrassed. Espey (1994) also writes of picking up street language near the canal where so much of the life of the city in Shanghai took place, and repeating phrases that turned out to be obscene, shocking his kindergarten teacher and somewhat inhibiting him from speaking Chinese (Shanghai dialect) for a long time afterward. Note that these stories, although unfortunate, have a humorous aspect, and the authors of these books tell them semi-humorously, hoping to entertain the reader. This tone is, perhaps, another sign that their speaking the language correctly wasn't really a high priority for them.

Espey did find that his knowledge of Shanghai Chinese was something he could use to conspire with friends or servants against some of the missionary adults, so in that case, language was a sort of power. However, that kind of power is trivial, only for fun, really, compared with the kind of power speakers of other languages are trying to attain through knowledge of English; the difference, once again, relates to one's privilege or lack thereof.

There are several mentions of local people's reactions to the MKs speaking local languages. Denton (2003: 76) states that *the Chinese all got a kick out of an American boy speaking their language*, and further says that in the Philippines, where his family had moved, he was *known as the Americano who spoke the dialect [Ilonggo] fluently* (p. 119).

A naïve but somewhat ugly language-related tendency of some of the MKs and even their parents was a tendency to make fun of the ways in which local people, especially in countries where colonial English was common, spoke English. In India, it was occasionally 'humorously' called 'Babu English' or simply 'chee-chee'. These terms indicated English with an Indian accent and intonation, and were usually said mockingly or condescendingly. I remember fellow MKs in India using the term 'chee-chee', and even mimicking that variety of English for 'humorous' effect; it is possible that I did so myself, although I don't remember it specifically. I don't remember adults correcting this joking about Indian accents, although again it is possible that they did and I have forgotten it.

Sometimes MKs' language learning led to trouble even after the MKs returned to North America. Lloret, who had become fluent in Spanish in Mexico, was scolded in his Spanish class in Florida during a furlough for not speaking the kind of Spanish from Spain that his teacher taught. Then language sometimes caused problems again when the MKs returned to the country where their parents worked; they had partly or completely forgotten their non-English language. Henderson-James (2009: 31), for example, upon returning to Angola at about age seven, was crestfallen to find that she *couldn't find the words in Portuguese. How did I say it? I was completely surprised to find I couldn't speak my almost natal language.*

I was somewhat taken aback by Orr's story of an MK friend's mother's ordering French records so her daughter could learn French; although the MK didn't learn local languages, she was encouraged to learn French. This indicates to me a sense that the local language was not important for the MKs to learn, as they would not use it in the long run after they returned to North America. Then I had the unsettling realization that I and my siblings and cohorts had done the same thing: we learned only a little of local languages, yet studied Latin and French at our boarding school.

Memoirists' Later Memories Regarding Local Languages

Although it would have been convenient for my thesis regarding privilege to find more explicit discussion of this issue in the memoirs, I did not find many overt explanations of not learning the local languages. The memoirists did not state that this was so because learning them was too much trouble, not necessary or just irrelevant to English-speaking children. They didn't state that they knew they could manage fine without them, because of their privileged statuses, or that they knew they would eventually return to the US or Canada, where speaking another non-Western language would not be particularly useful. Perhaps they considered these factors too obvious to state, or perhaps it just didn't enter their minds as an important topic.

However, I found the MKs' silences themselves rather meaningful. As mentioned earlier, many of the books simply did not mention learning or speaking local languages. There were almost no statements that it would be useful, appropriate, respectful to the country in which the MKs lived or enjoyable to learn those languages. A few mentioned regret at not learning local languages, but this was usually only briefly, even offhandedly, mentioned. For example, McMurdie (2009: 52), who had lived in the Philippines, said *During my childhood, much to my regret, I learned only a few polite Bicol phrases ... and more than a few rude phrases.* Harvey (2009: 35), who when talking to local people, sometimes used a mixture of English, French and African dialects, and *our own version of sign language*, rather wistfully mentions in her memoir that she wishes she had learned more of the Djimini dialect.

The attitudes of the MKs toward learning local languages were, with a few exceptions, somewhat blithe. They either didn't learn any, or didn't find such learning important enough to mention in their memoirs, or learned it and forgot it, or learned a bit and told humorous stories about it. Alter (1998: 125), for example, writes in a throwaway line, *Though I had grown up speaking the language [Hindi], I did not know how to read and write* until he was required to learn in his boarding school. (His school was an exception to what I said earlier about American schools' generally not teaching local languages.) I must note, though, that Alter, later in his memoir, was one of the very few to discuss a linguistic issue, that of the social significance of different personal pronouns in Hindi. Another who did so was Kuegler, writing about the difficulties of learning the Fayu language caused by its being a tone language. Alter was also one of the few to ponder with some sadness the likelihood that he would forget how to speak a local language, Hindi in his case, when he returned to the US.

This general lack of mention in most memoirs doesn't mean that it wasn't a good and important experience for those who did learn the languages, but it seems that they considered it good in the sense that (a) it was part of their childhood memories, along with all the other memories, and (b) it seemed like a good thing, an enriching thing, to learn the languages, but not important enough to put too much effort into it.

Language Learning and Privilege

This research sheds light on issues of social class and colonial privilege. As Johnston (2017: 155–156) puts it, 'Unequal language relations, in which one side learns the other's language but not vice versa, are typical of hegemonic and indeed colonial relations ... and the hegemony of

English is particularly marked'. He goes on to say that the English school in Poland that was his research site 'at times felt like a colonial enterprise'. As mentioned at the beginning of this chapter, MKs had the luxury, like other privileged populations, of *choosing* whether or not to learn additional languages, rather than being forced to by immigration status, education and work necessities, or other situations in which learners *must* learn languages for survival and advancement. When one has colonial and/or social class privilege, one can learn a language if one wants to, or ignore it if one doesn't feel like it, or take it up and drop it as it becomes convenient or pleasant or not. This privileged status contrasts with that of immigrant, refugee and international students studying English in North America and elsewhere. These populations do not have that same privilege; they need English in order to get the kinds of jobs they want, and in order to have any chance of attaining, or maintaining, membership in the middle or affluent social classes, whether in North America, in their own countries or elsewhere. English itself is a privileged language, and speakers of English are privileged too.

I, like a few of the memoirists, have some regrets about not learning local languages, or not learning them well, or forgetting them. Further, I regret the heedless way that I, my brothers, and many other missionary kids more or less dismissed the importance of learning and remembering the languages of the places we lived for many years of our childhood. The Telugu language, the one I learned when I was two years old, is still somewhere, in some form, in my head and heart, but I cannot retrieve it, except for a few words. It is tantalizingly just out of my reach, and thus sometimes haunts me. Once in a while a word or phrase will rise to the surface, sometimes during a dream, and becomes a remnant of nostalgia incarnated.

7 Gender

Throughout this book, I have focused on various themes found in the 42 missionary kid memoirs, with special attention to themes and supporting excerpts related to colonial aspects of the missionary project, and of the lives and experiences of the missionary kids. In this chapter and the next, still keeping in mind these colonial aspects, I turn to a brief overview of the gender, race and social class identities of the MKs, as well as those of others around them. I would have liked to write about sexual identity as well, but, perhaps unsurprisingly given the time period that most of the MKs are writing about (roughly the mid-20th century), none of the memoirists brought up this topic, except for one aforementioned lone, brief mention by Addleton of once seeing *hijira*s (male-to-female transsexuals). In this chapter, I address gender identities in the contexts of the MKs' parents' mission work and identities, their living in a country not their home country, the colonial history and the corresponding or contrasting identities of local people of the mission sites.

The MK identities (and those of their parents and of the local people) are, like everyone's identities, complex, multiple and fluid (Burke & Stets, 2009; Norton, 2000, 2013). Identities are also intersectional, as each identity affects each other one and creates a whole that is different from the sum of the parts (Hill Collins & Bilge, 2016; Crenshaw, 1991; Hancock, 2016).

I address gendered aspects of MKs' lives, including those related to themselves, their parents and the local people in the countries where they lived. Gender has been a salient factor in the missionary enterprise from the beginning, regarding missionaries, missionary kids and the people in the countries where the missionaries worked. Cunningham (quoted in Bowie, 1993: 1) noted that 'missionary work ... was clearly perceived as a task performed by men that women merely supplemented. Missionary was a male noun; it denoted a male actor, male action, male spheres of service'. Missionary kids, especially those living in other countries than their own in the early and middle periods of the 20th century, grew up with this background and understanding about the role of women missionaries, including their own mothers; they also had gendered views of the local people.

Women Missionaries' Contexts and Numbers

Some recent academic work has made the connection between imperialism and gender a particular focus. As Huber and Lutkehaus (1999: 1) put it,

> [T]he imperial mission was a gendered mission. This is not only because gender was a frequent idiom for relationships of power in the colonies, the imagery of empire often feminizing its subjects and creating of its agents super-men (Said 1978). Nor is it only because certain colonial policies specifically aimed to control or change relationships between women and men (Stoler 1991). Rather, what gives the colonies special significance in the history and sociology of gender is that the extreme circumstances created by empire so often placed pressure on received understandings about differences between the sexes and their proper roles among colonized and colonizers alike.

This increasing research about colonialism and gender provides a conceptual foundation for connections between missionary work and gender. Because it provides context for the beliefs and experiences of the MK memoirists, and because it provides evidence for the colonial influences on MK lives, I here begin with information about the roles of women missionaries throughout the years. Since the late 1970s, the topic of gender issues in mission work has been increasingly studied (e.g. Bowie *et al*., 1993; Huber & Lutkehaus, 1999; Hunter, 1984; Robert, 1996, 2014), partly simply to make the work of women missionaries, and that of the effects of missionary work on women, more visible. In fact, there have been women missionaries almost since the beginning of European and North American missionary work, although their presence and work have mostly been downplayed until recently. MacMillan (2007: 252) points out, regarding India specifically, 'The largest single group of women who worked in India were the missionaries. In 1911, for example, the census counted 1,236 European women in religious work throughout the country, as compared to 1,943 men'. Cox (2002: 153), writing of British missionaries in India and throughout the world, states wryly that

> [m]issionary narratives of male clerical heroism, which provide the foundation narratives for all subsequent histories of mission work, obscure the cooperative nature of an enterprise that involved extensive collaboration

between men and women at all levels from the very first days in Punjab. I have found that a simple assertion that two-thirds of British missionaries worldwide were women by 1900 continues to be greeted with surprise. By 1931, when the practice of counting married women as full missionaries had at last become entirely routine, 70 percent of the 622 Protestant foreign missionaries in northwest India were women.

Note the telling point that married missionary women were not counted as full missionaries until the early 20th century; before that, they were considered and classified simply as wives of missionaries. Similar statistics applied to female US missionaries. King (1989: 15) states that 'women represented forty-nine percent of all missionaries in 1830 and sixty percent in 1890'. Similarly, Hollinger (2017: 7) writes that in the mid 20th century, about two-thirds of missionary personnel were women and notes that '[missions afforded women opportunities to perform social roles often denied to them in the US'. Hollinger gives the example of women missionary physicians in India, who, by the 1950s, made up nearly half of all missionary physicians.

During the peak of the colonial enterprise, in the late 19th and early-to-mid 20th centuries, when some women in England and North America were starting to do jobs such as nursing and teaching, women started to be part of what was considered a 'civilizing mission' as missionaries. 'Missionary movements in several nations became increasingly feminized' in the late 19th century and beyond (Huber & Lutkehaus, 1999: 8). So the common tropes of missionary women as civilizing influences aided in women's acceptance and value to the mission project, but at the price of stereotypical views of women and of their supposed special virtues.

The Work of Women Missionaries

The missionary wives (and, as mentioned above, reflecting the gender norms of the first two-thirds of the 20th century, they were usually referred to as wives, rather than as co-equal missionaries) often did what was considered perhaps less essential (than that of male missionaries) supportive work, such as speaking and working with local women, and setting up women's Bible Study groups and related organizations. The 'single lady' missionaries did more extensive and various types of work; some of these were doctors, nurses or teachers. Some of them did what was termed 'women's work' (Allman, 1994; Haggis, 2000; Welch, 2005), working primarily or exclusively with local women, in a more focused and time-intensive way than the 'wives' were able to do.

Very few women missionaries, married or single, were ministers or pastors. One activity I remember from my own MK days was that women missionaries educated local Christian 'Bible women' (Kent, 1999) who would in turn go out and speak with other women about Christianity. However, in general missionary women were left out of the larger intellectual and theological work of the missionary enterprise. Flemming (1989: 1) notes that '[w]ell into the 20th century, church policy discouraged [missionary] women [in Asia] from participating in' work on 'changing theologies of mission and the development of governance structures in Asian churches'.

I feel compelled to add a personal note here: as a child and teenager in missionary communities in India, I greatly admired these strong and independent 'single lady' missionaries. In fact, I believe they were an influence on my budding feminist views, views that have been such an important part of my life ever since.

Reasons for Increasing Numbers of Women Missionaries

Although women's missionary work was less valued than that of men, one reason for the large number of women missionaries was that missionary work provided an opportunity and outlet for American women, and especially unmarried women, to do more interesting work and have more impact in their work than they would be allowed, normally, to do in the US and Canada. Hunter (1984: 35–36) points out that for many women,

> missionary work could ... blend the somewhat conflicting vocational [in the sense of religious] and professional needs female volunteers brought to it. Missionary service demanded a life commitment and paid for that commitment with a guarantee of modest economic security, opportunity for achievement abroad, and renown at home. Mission service offered women many of the gratifications of purpose, status, and permanence associated with the developing professions, without requiring the bold assault on female conventions demanded of the new 'professional' women.

Even those women who had already worked in North America often had had jobs with low pay and low status, such as secretaries or, most frequently, teachers. For teachers during the mid-19th century and into the 20th century, salaries were very low, and there were few opportunities for advancement. For a young woman looking at a lifetime of such conditions, or at minimum the years until she was married (when she would usually stop working), the excitement, status and sense of doing something important that missionary work offered were certainly attractive (Hunter, 1984).

Another reason for the increasing numbers of female missionaries was that missionary boards and male missionaries realized that men did not have access to preach, teach and in general minister to the local women, because of cultural norms prohibiting much contact between men and unrelated women. Women missionaries could fill this gap and do these various types of work with local women in a way that men could not. The early missionary educator Isabella Thorburn's brother brought her to India, where he was already a missionary, because he realized 'how very crippled missionary work must be when carried on by men alone' (Nalini, 2006: 269).

A third reason was that male missionaries felt they needed wives to run the domestic parts of their lives and to raise their children. In this instance, although many missionary wives actively worked in both spheres (missionary work and domestic duties), their single women missionary colleagues were able to focus their time and energy and talents more completely on the actual missionary work.

Still another aspect of the role of women missionaries is that some missionaries and others believed that women missionaries' example as role models in the domestic realm was part of their missionary work, and a way to influence local people and local culture. Flemming (1989: 2) labels this women's work as 'domestic evangelism', which was more discreet and indirect than the evangelical work of male missionaries. Women were also, relatedly, seen as 'civilizers' and 'characterize[ed] themselves as agents of change' (Flemming, 1989: 3). Hunter puts it as follows:

> Throughout the nineteenth century ... women relied particularly on 'blessed influence' rather than on direct authority to win compliance from other peoples. Their approach was intimate and personal rather than directive. They associated their Christian mission with their domestic responsibility to instill moral character ... and to breed refinement ... Their special concern with the details of domestic life made them both the most dedicated and the most successful emissaries of an entire civilization. (Hunter, 1984: xiv)

This last sentence is an extravagant claim, yet the claim was widely believed. It reinforces the ideas of Christianity that women are most effective in the domestic, and extended domestic, realms, as they quietly instill and reinforce religion and morality in their children and in others around them. Hunter's last sentence in the quotation above also reinforces the claims of postcolonial theory regarding the pervasive, many-tentacled aspect of colonial influences around the world. The essence of American (Western) civilization is perhaps conveyed more in day-to-day life than in the dramatics of sermons or of lifesaving medical work. The role of this cultural modeling is thus either highly effective or highly insidious, depending on one's viewpoint about colonialism and the spread of Christianity in countries and cultures that predominantly practice other religions.

Implications of Gendered Roles of Missionaries

Missionary women, whether because it was their first choice or whether they were limited in which kinds of missionary work they could do, mainly worked with women, and 'devoutly hoped that the lifelong, sacrificial efforts of women missionaries on behalf of women in the "heathen" lands of Asia, Africa and the Middle East would lead to real changes in those women's lives' (Flemming, 1989: 1). Despite the disturbing term 'heathen', and the colonial, imperial and gendered aspects of the women's work, there is something admirable and feminist (although the missionary women would be very unlikely to use this term) about this dedication to making a difference in the lives of women around the world. Some missionary women made the explicit claim that Christianity was emancipatory for women, and women in the American churches back in the US often supported missionaries partly because of this belief, supporting 'the women's foreign missionary movement as a strategy for social change on behalf of women' (King, 1989: 117). However, the feminist idea of women bonding with other women was seldom articulated; Flemming (1989: 6) notes that despite missionary women devoting their lives to working with local women, in both China and India there was very little sense of 'shared identity as *women*, i.e., sisterhood ... and their common allegiance to Christian doctrine was their only bond'. It is exactly these types of contradictions regarding colonialism and gender and feminism that riddle the work of missionaries and the analyses of those who study that work.

Missionaries, and MKs, as part of the larger world, experienced the same issues and discrimination regarding gender that others of their time periods did. Women missionaries had less power than men, and were considered as auxiliary in many ways. In a married missionary couple, the women were often not even paid. The single women missionaries had more power and better pay, but were still not considered as having the same status as the male missionaries. Robert (1996) describes the fears that male missionaries, as well as the males back home, had about women missionaries (and mission board members) having too much power and independence, which they considered wrong and unseemly. This concern was reinforced by a fundamentalist movement in the 1920s that believed that the Bible forbade women from being independent or having power. In consequence, some women's mission boards were dissolved (Robert, 1996). The work of female missionaries became de-emphasized, and was often 'officially unrecognized and unrecorded' (Huber & Lutkehaus, 1999: 13).

However, throughout the mission enterprise, there were contradictions and counter-narratives regarding gender and, in particular, regarding the role of female missionaries. Even when considered as auxiliary, or as 'wifely assistants', the husbands themselves 'repeatedly testified that they were able to devote themselves to their ministerial duties in large part because their wives attended to the more social needs of their target population – teaching children, nursing the sick, delivering babies, teaching domestic arts' (Thorne, 1999: 42).

Most of the research on gender issues among missionaries focuses on the missionaries themselves, rather than the local women they worked with. However, note has been made in missionary histories of the positions of local women in the countries where missionaries worked. Pruitt (2005) points out that missionaries, especially female missionaries, focused largely on the oppression of local women, as manifested by female infanticide, arranged marriages, subjugation to husbands, confinement to home ('zenana' in Brahman homes in India) and/or the terrible position of widows (in India, for Hindus, even being required to kill themselves, in the ritual called 'sati'). All of these practices and attitudes were labeled as 'Oriental' and 'heathen'. 'Oriental' women were also labeled as idle, dirty and uneducated, and these were pointed to as indexes to their immorality (Pruitt, 2005). All of these conditions and characterizations gave impetus to women missionaries, and their mission boards, to see their work as helping these 'heathen' women, through schools and medical aid, and through setting examples of how Christian women and families should exist and comport themselves. Pruitt calls the work of 19th century evangelicals 'evangelical Orientalism' (Pruitt, 2005: 4). On a more positive note, Lankina and Getachew (2012: 105) report on research on the role of missionaries in increasing female education in India. Using the case of the state of Kerala, 'India's most progressive state when it comes to female education', these authors demonstrate that

> Kerala illustrates how prior to the arrival of Protestant Christian missions, native governments and established religious groups showed limited interest in female education outside of a narrow elite. By the end of the nineteenth century, following activity by Protestant missions, they had become strong advocates of mass, including female, education, and key education providers. (Lankina & Getachew, 2012: 105–106)

The Memoirists' Perspectives on Gender

Although the memoirists do not discuss gender issues extensively, some aspects of gender can be seen in their portrayals of their settings, the way they saw their mothers' and fathers' areas of work and status levels, and what they saw of gender relations in the countries where their families lived.

The MKs' parents, like other missionaries, as noted above, mostly replicated the gendered job divisions of their countrypeople 'back home'. The memoirists' fathers were mostly ministers, doctors or administrators. The memoirists' mothers were teachers, leaders of women's groups at churches and assistants. The mothers often worked only part-time in these jobs, as they, like North American women at home during the mid-20th century, devoted much of their time and energy to their children and homes, and to being helpmeets to their husbands. This was true of my own mother; she worked part-time in mission schools and in the mission hospital, more as an advisor than as a regular worker. She worked with Bible women and with women's groups in the local church. All of this was important and time-consuming work. However, she needed to spend much of her time raising four children (especially before we were old enough to go to boarding school) and running a household. The latter was complicated by the lack of 'modern conveniences' (a fraught phrase in this context), and even of running water and, at times, electricity. Granted, there were servants to help, but it was still difficult work. The home was mainly her responsibility (replicating the pattern in North America and, mostly, around the world; my father's work as a physician and administrator was always paramount).

It is not surprising that North American women whose own work and status was somewhat devalued by society would make similar judgments about the local women. Some memoirists recall their parents' casually sexist (sometimes, demonstrating intersectionality, tinged with racist) beliefs and comments. Maybury, for example, quotes from a letter from her mother, Hilda, speaking disparagingly and condescendingly of the women who worked in her garden for about 5 cents a day:

> If we had two or three gardeners they could do as much work as all these women, who sit gossiping, or work with a baby on their hip, or wander off to eat chapatis! At least it keeps them from starvation ... It is impossible to hurry them. (Maybury, 2011: 119)

Note that, for Hilda, the only 'true' gardeners were men.

The memoirists themselves, as children and teenagers, also learned the gender expectations of their time periods. Boys tended to have more vigorous adventures. Orr, a female memoirist, writes that the MK boys she knew were sometimes violent toward animals, such as swinging a cat around by its tail. She speculated that *[p]erhaps something of the great white hunter mentality had been communicated to my male peers, who found plenty of flora and fauna in Nigeria to extinguish* (Orr, 2003: 79). Schoonmaker (2011: 5) also confirmed this outdoors/hunting aspect of many MK boys' experiences, writing at length of a hunting trip in India with his father and other missionary fathers and sons, *men and boys only*. Boys were also more concerned about presenting masculine images, even from a young age. Coleman (2003: 51), when he first went to boarding school as a very young boy, was concerned not to *make the mistake of wearing a shirt that made me look like a girl*. Boys had more freedom to play outside with local boys, which allowed them a closer connection with local people, local land and local languages. Schroeder (2013: 53), for example, as mentioned in Chapter 6, points out that *girls didn't play outside as much as their brothers, so didn't learn Amharic nearly as well*. Girls were more limited in what they were allowed to do, and acted out their feelings in different ways; Orr, for instance, had a hard time with transitions, especially the one back to the US, and dealt with her feelings through an eating disorder.

It is important to remember, however, one of the aspects of intersectionality: one type of privilege often counteracts, at least to some extent, a different type of lack of privilege. MK girls, because of their colonial privilege, their white privilege and their class privilege, had certain freedoms and recognitions among the local people that might not be available back in North America. Orr (2003: 220) tells of how she and other young MK girls were given the position of leading the *outdoors Nigerian male staff in devotionals on Saturday mornings*. As an adult writing her memoir, she wonders how the men felt about this: did they like it? Did they feel they had to accept it in order to keep their jobs? Did they laugh about it afterwards? We can imagine that it was somewhat galling for these men, although they outwardly accepted it as a condition of their employment.

The memoirists, as children, absorbed the sexist attitudes they observed, even applying them to their own families, in particular their mothers. Henderson-James (2009: 99), for example, remembers that

> *I unconsciously drank in the prevailing patriarchal Portuguese culture. Not knowing why, I cringed in embarrassment over any public acts of my mother. When she spoke Portuguese or Umbundu in a group, it took all my will to keep from clamping my hands over my ears, to shut out her ungainly accent, her weak woman's voice. Though the Angolans and Portuguese we knew were never anything but polite, I felt safer when my father was the focus of attention.*

Henderson-James seems embarrassed and offended that her mother draws attention to herself, which she seems to feel is inherently unfeminine. However, she also critiques her mother for being too feminine ('her weak women's voice'). Henderson-James obviously craves the more desirable characteristics she perceives that males have, and goes on to say that she and her female friends took male names for fun, not surprisingly believing that *becoming boys lent us power and status* (Henderson-James, 2009: 155).

With the advantage of age and time, some memoirists, looking back, were more understanding of gender issues and sexism. Addleton, for instance, writes of the different situations for female and male MKs growing up in Pakistan. He points out that boys were able to roam and play freely, whereas girls were much more restricted in where, or how far afield, they could go, and in what they could do.

A few of the writers note the role of women in the countries where they lived as MKs. Looper (2008: 132) summarizes her observations as follows:

> *The African cultures were strongly patriarchal with clearly delineated roles for men and women. When a couple was in public together, the woman always walked a few steps behind the man. He would stride along carrying his spear or a club, while the woman carried their goods in a bundle balanced on her head.*

Looper also discusses marriage customs among the Mossis. However, the extent and level of discussion of gender among the local people in the countries where the MKs grew up is quite limited in the memoirs.

Turning to the present day, gender equity is unfortunately still an issue in some mission settings. Johnston (2017: 160), for example, points out that the female heads of the evangelical school in Poland that was Johnston's research site often struggled 'against authorities that did not accept such an active and independent role for women in the research field'; and Walters (2007) writes of a missionary woman whose husband left her while they were on furlough in the US, and who became destitute because the mission board paid their joint salary only to the husband. The same mission board ruled that, after the couple divorced, the woman, who wanted to go back to her mission work, could not do so as a divorced woman, even though the divorce was not her fault.

Fortunately, some matters related to gender equality have improved since the days of the memoirists on the mission field. Regrettably, on the other hand, many such matters and issues still exist.

8 Race and Social Class

As I wrote in the prior chapter about gendered aspects of MKs' lives, in this chapter I write about racial and social class aspects of their lives, as well as those of their parents and of local people in the countries where they lived. Both race and class are identities that underlie almost everything about the colonial enterprise, and consequently underlie the missionary enterprise as well. As always, these identities intersect with each other and with other identities.

One relevant example of these intersecting identities is the ambiguities of race, complexified by the ambiguities of social class, as manifested in British India during the Raj. A vast majority of the British who served in India were white, and worked in India for periods of time but still went back and forth to England, and generally retired there. However, some of them were economically disadvantaged, and eventually ended up living in India as their primary home; these were labeled the 'domiciled community' (Mizutani, 2011: 1). An overlapping group of British were those who were the result of relationships with local people, Indians, and were labeled Euroasian. Mizutani (2011: 2) argues that these two groups brought about a view of whiteness as 'equivocal', 'complex and even contradictory' (Mizutani, 2011: 219). He states, pointing out the intersections of race and social class in this setting, that

> [d]espite the [British] government's desire to make it appear otherwise, the white population of India turned out to be disturbingly heterogeneous, particular in terms of intra-communal hierarchies of race ('unmixed or not'), class ('middle class or not') and domicile ('reared and educated in the metropole or not').

Racial and class identities manifested themselves in various other ways in the missionary contexts, and specifically in the MK memoirs.

Race

Before looking at race in the context of white missionaries in other countries, it is important to look at the history in the US. During the days of slavery, the churches tried to convert slaves to Christianity. Some did so because they genuinely believed the slaves would be better off as Christians, and because they wanted to extend the numbers of Christians. However, as Stevens (2012b: 7) points out, this effort was sometimes motivated by the self-serving belief that 'a Christian slave was a better servant'. Stevens also notes that this evangelizing effort put slaves in an even more difficult position, in that, if they converted, they may be treated better by their 'owners', but they may also be ostracized by fellow slaves and free blacks, who would consider them to have abandoned their African culture. So the context of missionaries' work with slaves, and later free people of color, both in the US and elsewhere, was complex, colonial and instrumental.

Although the great majority of North American missionaries were white, there were a very few African-American missionaries to other countries. One of the first was George Liele, who was born a slave, converted to Christianity, ministered to and taught other slaves, was freed by his master to allow him to do Christian work, and went to Jamaica in 1783 to do mission work there. This was 'ten years before Englishman William Carey launched the modern foreign missions movement' when he went to India in 1794 (Sidwell, 2012: 9). After the Civil War, the African Methodist Episcopal Church and other African-American churches started to send some missionaries outside of the US. Walls (2012: 25) states that '[t]he Christianization of Africa was the dream of the African-American Church', and most of the small number of African-American missionaries went to Africa. Possibly the best known of these was William Henry Sheppard, a Southern Presbyterian missionary in the Congo, where 'he gained fame for helping to expose King Leopold II's depredations against the Congolese' (Hollinger, 2017: 12). Since that time, there has been a very small but definite presence of African-American missionaries in Africa and elsewhere. Stevens (2012a: 230) believes that African-American missionaries are 'in a position to become one of the most effective mission forces in the world today'. There have also been North American missionaries of Asian and other racial and ethnic backgrounds, but also very few. The vast majority of North American missionaries to other countries have been white.

Missionaries' racial attitudes

Race was always a fraught issue for white missionaries. Not surprisingly, they brought their racial attitudes from North America, just as the British had brought theirs from England, and these included, throughout

American history, racial stereotypes and prejudice. Hunter, writing of missionaries in the early 20th century in China, says that '[m]issionaries ... assumed the superiority of their own Caucasian, Anglo-Saxon stock to the other racial blendings of the world, and they sometimes arrived on the mission field expecting to be greeted by an alien form of humanity' (Hunter, 1984: 161). Crowder (1968, as quoted in Okon, 2014), speaking of the African context, agrees, stating that

> Christian Europe ... felt itself morally superior to heathen Africa ... this sense of moral superiority was reinforced by theories of racial superiority which placed the white man at the top of the hierarchy, the black man at the bottom. Thus the European colonial powers found nothing wrong in occupying and ruling lands belonging to African peoples. (Okon, 2014: 202–203)

Further, Johnston (2003: 9) argues that 'missionaries sought to consolidate their precarious position in colonial cultures by mimicking stereotypical imperial practices, of racial superiority for example, and by rigidly enforcing and encouraging colonial versions of them in their "heathen" charges'. Some overt signs of such racial aspects of imperialism were the ways that local people were required to call the missionaries by such titles as 'sahib' or 'bwana'.

However, missionaries and their children soon and often spoke of *not* being prejudiced, and asserted how much they loved the local people and were not even conscious of the racial differences. I am reminded of how still, in the early 21st century, there is much racial prejudice in the US and elsewhere and, on the part of those who feel they are not prejudiced, much denial of even noticing race ('I am colorblind', and 'I don't care if a person is red, yellow, black or white'). Despite their protests otherwise, '[m]issionaries were proud of their racial backgrounds and sometimes explained that their idealistic sense of mission was a result of superior natural selection within their own race' (Hunter, 1984: 163) (thus displaying a mixture of racism and classism). They seemed to feel, almost by definition of missionary work, that their white and 'civilized' superiority obligated them to 'help' the inferior local people. Much of this was unconscious and often well-intentioned, although no less problematic, paternalism that drew on racism.

These attitudes of the racial superiority of Europeans and Americans in the mission field in specific were often seen in the interactions of missionaries and other personnel in the local churches. In India, for example, there was an attempt to build churches and church-related organizations that were run by local people. The ultimate goal was that Indians would run Indian churches. However, during that process, there was a sort of tug-of-war between the white missionaries and the Indians about power, authority, resources, pay and other factors. Although there was goodwill on both sides, there were tensions, many arising from unconscious racism and imperialism. As Cox (2002: 100) puts it, the Indian ministers and other leaders in the church felt that 'there was subordination. They could see the imperial fault lines, and they could see the gratifications of racial superiority'. Some missionaries tried to understand the Indians' points of view, but others were 'shocked and infuriated by accusations of paternalism or racism' (Cox, 2002: 101).

All of this was complicated by the fact that, in some countries at least, there were local forms of racism already, forms that the missionaries had to grapple with in their understanding of the country and people they were working with. For example, the caste system in India was and is a form of racism in many ways, one of which being that the people in the higher castes tend to be lighter-skinned than those in the lower castes. Indians are often open about their preference for lighter skin, such as in their newspaper and other advertisements for suitable matches for marriage. There is also a sense that the Tamil people of South India, who tend to have darker skin than many of the people in North India, are somewhat inferior for that reason. So the missionaries struggled with their own racism as well as that of the local people, although they took different forms.

Intersections of race with gender

As noted in Chapter 7 regarding intersectionality, a person may well have privilege granted by one or more aspects of their identities and lack privilege because of one or more other aspects. An interesting intersection between race and gender in the mission context is described by Margaret Sobel, who notes that European (white) women missionaries 'played ambiguous roles as members of a sex considered to be inferior within a race that considered itself superior' (quoted by Huber & Lutkehaus, 1999: 18). These 'memsahibs', as they were called in India, and equivalently titled women missionaries in other countries, were a truly complex mixture of powerful and powerless.

Interestingly, Thorne (1999: 52) shows that, in the British context, feminists often came from religious and specifically evangelical families and backgrounds, and these backgrounds influenced nascent feminists to believe in 'global sisterhood'. These feminists'connections to British empire were displayed, for example, in missionary tracts that 'appealed explicitly to women's solidarity across "racial" divides by condemning the patriarchal abuse of heathen women in the colonies. Missionary literature abounded with "heart-rending details" of female infanticide, child marriage, forced prostitution, polygamy, widow burning, and the like' (Thorne, 1999: 52). The missionaries' views about poor 'heathen' women of various races in various countries displayed the intersectionality discussed above, and although these views were signs of generosity and caring, they were also signs of racial and religious stereotyping and condescension.

The memoirists' views on race

As mentioned earlier, all of the memoirists in this study (and the vast majority of North American missionary families) are white. Most of the people in the countries where their parents did their missionary work were and are people of color. Because of widespread white privilege, even in countries where most people are of color, there was immediately and consistently a power dynamic in which the missionaries were perceived as, and perceived themselves as, having more power than (most of) the local people. As described in Chapter 4, MKs' attitudes and behaviors toward servants and other local people revealed their conscious or unconscious sense of white superiority.

White privilege was and is inextricably linked with colonial power, even after the original European and other colonists no longer technically held power. This continuing influence of colonialism has been called coloniality (Mignolo, 2011; Quijano, 2007). It is also intertwined with social class and economic privilege, further discussed below. However, the missionaries and their children were often either unaware of this power disparity or in denial about it, or didn't consider it important in the context of their work. In addition, most missionaries tended to be somewhat conservative politically and socially, and along with that perspective came the same racial assumptions and stereotypes that have been a longtime feature of American life and society. Even those who were open and caring, as called for by Jesus and the Christian religion, still often had the perspective that the local people were like children who needed education and enlightenment.

Some of the memoirists do write about race. Early on, some noticed racial differences, but didn't feel them to be important; to be able not to notice is of course a privilege in itself. Van Valkenburg (2014: 78), for example, says that *we were the only white people living in Sayaboury. In my mind, I never felt any different from Laotians.* Another such assertion comes from Orr (2003: 148), who writes that *I did not think of myself as*

American or as *Nigerian or even as an MK*. Others realized sooner that racial differences would be more consequential as they got older, and wrote about their dawning ideas about the differences between themselves and the local people regarding race. Coleman describes how he, as he started school, gradually realized that he and his preschool (Ethiopian) playmates, Zenebech and Mulugeta, would now take diverging paths. They would learn different languages and lead different lives. They had different kings and different Gods. *They had brown skin; I had pink* (Coleman, 2003: 73). Occasionally a memoirist used a racist label that is now considered unacceptable, but at the time it was not. Cordell (2008: 11), for example, in writing about her time in India in the early 20th century, speaks of someone as a '*sturdy little Jap*'.

Some, with the vantage point of time and retrospection, see the racial issues more clearly than most. Henderson-James (2009: 99), for example, describes her complicated reactions to her time in Angola as follows:

> *The oppressive atmosphere impelled me, a child with an emerging political consciousness, to divide the world into black and white, love and hate. Loyalty to black Angolans came to mean hatred of white Portuguese. But, in fact, I was dancing between complex alliances of race, nationality, gender, and religion. I constantly had to shift and shuffle my loyalties.*

She goes on to say, perceptively, that because of these shifting and unpredictable alliances, *My white skin protected me, while my American citizenship imperiled me* (Henderson-James, 2009: 99).

However, among the MKs there was generally a lack of awareness, and/or a glib, even blithe, lack of understanding about the ways in which racial prejudices worked, and about the consequences of such prejudices. One striking example of cluelessness is Kopp's (2014: back cover) statement that *Africa was my playground*, and his flip question, *Who said an African-American has to be black?*

As with gender, some of the racial issues in the colonial missionary world still cast a long shadow on the relatively decolonized world of the mid-20th century during which most of the memoirists were MKs. The old beliefs and feelings in the racial superiority of whites have psychological remnants in the cultures, literatures and behaviors of both white and non-white countries and individuals; these remnants still have real consequences.

Social Class

Social class too was a factor in the lives of missionaries and their children. The missionaries that were recruited by mission boards and organizations in England and North America in the late 19th and early-to-mid-20th century were most often middle class (Bowie, 1993). They were generally highly educated, with graduate degrees in theology, medicine, education and other fields. Often missionaries, like many charitable workers at home, wanted to help the people in the countries where they were sent as missionaries, but also condescended to local people on the mission fields, considering them lower than themselves socially. Although it is true that, almost always, the economic status of the local people was lower, the label of low social class was unfortunately extended to a more generalized belief in essentially lower status and lower abilities. Thorne (1999) points out, again in the British context but easily seen in the North American missionary context as well, and here referring to missionary women but describing a phenomenon that applied to male missionaries as well, that

> [t]he 'gift' of missionary benevolence thereby validated colonial social hierarchies ... Whatever benefits colonized women may have accrued from missionary interventions (Brownfoot 1990), British women almost invariably emphasized their own dominance in the missionary gift exchange. They were, at the very least, elder sisters or, more often, maternal substitutes who 'cared' from the great distance of space, culture, and power inscribed in their discourse of moral character. (Thorne, 1999: 52)

Although the situations of British and American missionaries are sometimes discussed together in this book, it is of note that one memoirist, Schroth, opined that, at least in India, the British *generally consider themselves to be a higher class than [American] missionaries; [t]hey are like the Brahmins and we the outcastes* (Schroth, 2011: 100).

One small but significant symbol of social class and status was that not only the adult missionaries but also their children were often given honorary titles. Alter writes of how he and his brothers grew up in India as sahibs (an honorary term): *Stevie sahib, Joey sahib* and *Andy sahib*. He goes on to say, *That's what we were called by our cooks, bearers, ayahs, gardeners, and sweepers ... As children we took these titles for granted, as if they were simply part of our names ... we accepted this title from others and played the role* (Alter, 1998: 101).

Missionary families were in an unusual position regarding social class and economic status. When they were 'in the field' overseas, they had class and economic privilege (almost always along with and enhanced by racial privilege) because they were supported by mission boards or churches or individual sponsors back in North America. They had decent housing, clothing, food, education and transportation; in fact, compared with the vast majority of local people, their living conditions were luxurious. Missionaries' education and power were displayed in their setting up and administering of churches, schools and hospitals. In contrast with the lives and resources of local people, the missionaries seemed to be wealthy and of high social status. Some MKs were very aware of this difference, although not perhaps the extent of it. On the one hand, they would sometimes show off their toys, as my brothers and I did, I am embarrassed to say (Vandrick, 1999a). On the other hand, they noticed the differences. Coleman (2003: 132), for example, noted the gap between the living standards of the missionaries and the Ethiopians he knew. He says that *my friends' houses had dirt floors and ours had polished cedar*, and he reflects sadly about the differences. Orr (2003: 117) speaks more matter of factly about these class differences, saying *Of course I knew that my family was much wealthier than most Nigerians*. One of my own memories is of being shocked when one of the Indian church women, well-educated and an important personage in the church and community where we lived, told me (nicely, but wanting to educate me) that I perhaps didn't understand how lucky I was, and that she, for example, could not even afford toothpaste. I felt chastened, as I realized how much I took for granted.

Carolyn Servid (2000), an MK whom I knew in India, notes that, despite her fondness for, and connection with, local people who worked at her mission's hospital and at her family's home, and members of the local church, she had to acknowledge the differences.

> [I]n spite of their kindness, in spite of the affections they nurtured in me, I had to grow into the fact that I was not one of them. I was undeservedly privileged. I lived in the big house. My father was the hospital superintendent, my mother the head technician in the lab. We were Americans. We always had the option of an escape from India's discomforts – from poverty and disease, the disarray and inconveniences of an underdeveloped country. (Servid, 2000: 8)

Servid's sentence 'I was undeservedly privileged' gets to the crux of the matter, the uncomfortable truth about the missionary enterprise and the larger colonial enterprise. Bonk (2007) writes of how the (comparative, at least) affluence of missionaries widens the gap between them and the local people. He gives the example of missionaries in Kenya; I quote his description at length because, sadly, it vividly captures the 'divide':

> Western missionaries on the station were virtually isolated from their closest African neighbors ... It was a world apart – a world of privileged, indulged missionary children enjoying the best education that money can buy in that country; a world of industrious, supremely secure white

missionaries, spending their lives in worthwhile medical, educational, and developmental programs on behalf of poor Africans; a world of Western families, each with its glowing future; a world viewed by its closest neighbors with no little bitterness, envy, resentment, and sometimes naked hostility. (Bonk, 2007: 56)

Servid (2000) touches on another sensitive matter when she notes that missionaries were sometimes welcomed for their contributions to the local economies, but without the local people's necessarily being concomitantly pleased about their presence or their religious message. She says about Kodaikanal, where the school we both attended was located, that '[o]ur community was a little Anglo-American enclave catered to by the Indians of the town who must have appreciated the economic advantages we offered more than the spiritual benefits of our religious colonialism' (Servid, 2000: 29).

However, to complicate matters regarding social class privilege, missionaries back home in North America for furloughs mostly lost the privilege they had had in the mission field. Buettner (2004) wrote about British colonial families of the Raj living at a higher level than that from which they came in England. She points out that returning home to England 'often proved a letdown since it meant giving up the elevated standing based on class, race, and nationality they had enjoyed in India' (Buettner, 2004: 20). A similar phenomenon occurred for missionary families. Alter (1998: 144) perhaps best captures the contrast. *In India I was used to living a privileged and comfortable life, not lavish, but certainly more secure and wealthy than most of the people around us.* However, this changed when Alter's family returned to the US. *For the first time in my life it seemed that we were poor and I felt cheated and deprived* (Alter, 1998: 145). Orr (2003: 258), among other memoirists, makes the same point, but in her case with a racial twist: her family was wealthy in Nigeria, but back in the US, *we were the ones living on the edge of poverty, receiving welfare from the white folks* (presumably the churches that support missionaries). She, white herself, felt that she got a small glimpse of how the black Africans she knew must feel accepting charity from the white missionaries. The economic and social class contrasts between the MKs' lives on the mission field and back in North America are reminiscent of those of British lives as missionaries or as any part of the colonial enterprise on other continents. Many British and other European colonials went abroad in order to enhance their status, employ servants and in general escape their less elevated social status back home. In the case of the missionaries, I do not contend that they became missionaries to enhance their social status, but they did experience an elevated status in

India, Nigeria, Ethiopia and the other countries where they served as missionaries.

Several of the other memoirists, as well as my own family's experience, also indicated that, when missionary families went 'home' on furlough, they were often on very tight budgets. Furthermore, they had to spend much of their furlough time speaking at churches and asking for money for support of their work and their families. They were also given or sent packages with food and hand-me-down clothing. Even after they left the mission field, missionary families were far behind other families of the same education and social status (generally middle-class), because they had no savings, owned no houses, and had to restart their careers, often at a lower level than their experience justified.

Sometimes missionary children felt that they were treated by the home churches as poor relations. In Catherine Palmer's (2002) novel about missionary children, *The Happy Room*, a sarcastic conversation between MK siblings includes the following:

> 'If you are a missionary', Julia was saying, imitating her mother's voice, 'you can only buy your clothes off sale racks or get them at the secondhand store. On furlough [time back in the US], you wear other people's hand-me-down winter coats' ... 'We had hand-me-down Christmas trees, of course', Julia continued ... 'People's leftover, broken ornaments. Their half-melted candles. But, of course, we were just grateful, grateful, grateful. Oh, and then they'd send boxes of their used clothing all the way to Africa. Stained blouses. Ripped hems ... Yay, I get to wear somebody's sweat-stained bra. Whoopee'. (Palmer, 2002: 280–281)

Despite these setbacks for some, the families' essential middle-class status and the attributes and privileges it provided them did not disappear. For example, the MKs generally got excellent educations in their boarding schools, and despite some difficulties (and worse) experienced by some children there, did very well in school back in North America. Dow (2003) reports on research that shows that MK boarders scored an average of 100 points above the American average on the SAT (the test used by many American universities for decisions on admission), that 90–95% of MK boarding school graduates attended college, and that 74–81% graduated; these statistics are much higher than those for the average American population.

As with other identities, some of the memoirists understood these matters and these disparities better than others, although generally not until they were older. One of the more thoughtful memoirists,

Henderson-James, recalls her perceptions of social and economic inequalities as follows:

> *I was struck by how unfair life was. I wished I understood why we ourselves had a big, substantial house of cement and stucco with large, high-ceilinged rooms full of furniture ... And why we had electricity, cold running water, bathtubs, and toilets. And why we had all the food we wanted. And why my little brothers were healthy and not in danger of dying from diarrhea ... And why the dead baby's family had so little.* (Henderson-James, 2009: 96)

Another memoirist, Seaman, also thoughtful in his analysis of social class and economic differences, remembers that he prided himself on being more aware and caring than others whom he characterizes as 'ugly Americans'.

> *We proudly distinguished ourselves from the 'ugly Americans' in the Foreign Service and international businesses, disdaining their lives of luxury and aloofness from the 'real' Pakistan. But the essential characteristics of an expatriate lifestyle – practiced by almost all Westerners living in Third World countries – are the same: privilege, status, and an artificially high standard of living (in contrast to both the local population and what could have been afforded in one's home country). We were not immune to the attitudes inevitably bred in such a situation. It was hard not to feel superior.* (Seaman, 1997: 126)

I do not claim that attitudes about race and social status were worse among missionaries and MKs than among other North Americans. Yet it seems that being part of the mission project brought out these prejudices in particular ways that strikingly echoed those evident in the larger colonial enterprise.

9 Implications

The 'missionary kid' memoirs in this study relate the childhoods of MKs during the 20th century, especially the mid-century. Missionary life, and life in general, have changed since then in many ways. Although there are definitely still Christian missionaries, their ways of operating are somewhat different now. For example, now most missionaries go on short-term missions rather than as career missionaries. Also, rather than missionaries going from North America and Europe to other countries, or from the Global North to the Global South (although as noted earlier, these terms, like their predecessors such as First and Third Worlds, developed and developing countries, are problematic), there are many missionaries who go from and to non-Western countries.

Despite these changes, many of the issues illustrated in the memoirs, and analyzed in this book, continue to manifest themselves. How have the issues evolved, and what are the implications of those issues? In this concluding chapter, I briefly outline a small selection of topics that cluster around the continued and even accelerated spread of Western religion, language and culture, all still strongly embedded in the colonial enterprise and in its residual coloniality.

In particular I want to note that the spread of the English (and other European) languages has always been part of colonialism and of missionary work. Kachru (1995: 291) states bluntly and unequivocally that '[t]he English language is a tool of power, domination and elitist identity'. Pennycook and Makoni (2005) outline connections among these three elements: colonialism, missionary work and languages. They point out that missionary work has been part of the spread of English, sometimes to the detriment of local languages. They also point out that '[o]n the other hand, missionary linguists have played a particular role in the construction and invention of languages around the world' (Pennycook & Makoni, 2005: 137), and go on to describe ways in which this can be both beneficial and very harmful.

I do not claim to address these issues comprehensively, but I do want to sketch out some of the connections between the past, as revealed in the memoirs in this study, and the present. Scholars, governmental and non-governmental organizations, activists, parents and others struggle with the kinds of knotty, complex sociopolitical issues addressed here. Questions of religion, language, culture, education and relationships among different groups of people are some of the central questions of our time.

Exoticizing the 'Other'

As discussed in Chapter 3, the 'missionary kid' memoirists often write about phenomena and events that they consider, and expect that their readers will consider, unusual and exotic. They emphasize matters that are different from those in North America, such as wild animals, 'unusual' food (i.e. food that is not commonly eaten in North America), 'strange' customs, rare illnesses and 'fascinating' rituals and ceremonies found in Asia, Africa and South America. The MKs enjoy feeling that they experienced exciting lives full of the 'exotic', and they play up this aspect. In contrast, immigrants and international students are in effect considered *to embody* the 'exotic' when they are studying in North America, and most often want to avoid being regarded this way. For example, immigrants and international students are often asked by North Americans whom they meet, and by their teachers and fellow students, about their foods and customs. This focus has been labeled by many teachers as the 'Foods and Festivals' approach to teaching language and culture. Students may enjoy sharing these aspects of their countries and cultures, but also may feel ambivalent about being positioned as exotic and 'other' (although they may not yet have the English vocabulary to explain their feelings this way).

In both cases, that of the people that the MKs met abroad, and that of international students and immigrants in North America, the non-American cultures and practices, as well as the non-American or newly American people themselves, are positioned as, and offer the *frisson* of, the exotic. This positioning, although unintentional, leads to or exacerbates an 'us' and 'them' dynamic. One culture (the dominant one, or at least the one with a history of domination, often colonial) is centered and the others are marginalized, positioned as 'different' and 'other'.

In the case of North American English language classes (or other types of classes for newcomers, such as 'orientations' or 'citizenship' classes), lessons about the 'foods and festivals' (and related topics about culture and society) of the students' original countries usually focus not only on the details of the various cultural practices, but also on comparing them with 'American' (North American, especially the US) culture. Thus, American culture is centered, and everything else is marginalized and defined in relationship to the center. Instructors believe that the 'foods and festivals' approach will allow students to showcase their own cultures, and make them more comfortable by giving them a familiar topic to discuss. These are laudable motivations, but the approach emphasizes stereotypes and 'difference' (Knight, 2008; Ladson-Billings, 1994; Vandrick, 2017).

In addition, these topics are often awkwardly introduced with questions about how these aspects of life and culture are in 'your country' or 'your culture', and with questions of how they differ from those in the US and Canada (or other English-dominant countries). Or, in classes with students with various backgrounds, they are asked to compare cultural practices from 'their countries' with each other. Although these are matters the students know about, they may feel uncomfortable discussing them in class, for fear that the differences will be considered by others to be strange or odd, or even deficiencies. These questions ask for a sort of performance as representative of one's country or culture that may feel risky, not only in front of students and instructors from other cultures, but even, or maybe especially, in front of students from one's own background. These problems are exacerbated by the assumption that everyone from a certain country has the same foods and festivals, customs and practices.

The 'foods and festivals' approach and discourses (in other words, the exoticizing of 'other' cultures) raise other issues as well. One is that generalizations about how things are done in the US, or 'in America', are also problematic, in the very multicultural and diverse country that the US is. The approach frames students, even immigrant students who may have lived in the US a long time, as being from another culture, and does not allow or reflect the common reality that these students often embody a blend of cultures, including 'American culture' as it is popularly portrayed. (Young people are often the first to pick up the latter.) Another factor is that immigrants and international students vary so widely in their backgrounds, including their economic and social class statuses, that again it is difficult to make generalizations about any group. For example, with today's globalization, students who come to the US as immigrants or – especially – international students are often from affluent or at least middle-class backgrounds, and thus have been exposed to international travel, or at least to American shops, restaurants, name brand clothing and technological products. So the differences among cultures have flattened out, especially for those from the international and prosperous elite (Vandrick, 2011b).

The larger and most disturbing context for the issues discussed above is the way that many Western scholars (both in Applied Linguistics/ELT and in other fields) and others in the general populace in the West often essentialize the cultures of non-Western countries, thus promoting Othering of those cultures, countries and the people who are from there. Kubota (1999: 9), for example, makes this point through the example of how Japanese culture is framed and constructed by Western scholars, giving many examples of such framings as the assumptions that Japanese culture values 'groupism, harmony, and deemphasis on critical thinking and self-expression'. She argues that 'the cultural dichotomy promoted in the applied linguistics literature is constructed by discourse that reflects and creates particular power relations in which the dominant group defines the subordinate group as the exotic Other' (Kubota, 1999: 11). Kubota points out the parallels between the types of Othering that occur in colonial discourse and these assumptions about Japanese culture.

Treatment of the 'Other'

I write in Chapter 4 of ways in which missionaries and their children often treated local people, especially their servants, with a sort of benign but nonetheless unjust and sometimes harmful condescension. Local people were patronized and sometimes even gently mocked, either to their faces or during family conversations about them. Somewhat similarly, both immigrants and international students in North America often experience being treated as if they are inferior, or at least marginalized. Some of this has to do with language issues; I will never forget one of my South American students many years ago telling me, with obvious pain and some anger, that because he did not speak English well, many Americans treated him as if he were a child. The marginalization and condescension also have to do with the insularity and (whether conscious or unconscious) assumptions of superiority of many North Americans, especially white North Americans. The consequences for the international students, especially those still studying English as a Second Language and/or English for Academic Purposes, can be the experiencing of a series of microaggressions. People from non-North American countries, and/or their children, especially those who are not white, are often regarded with suspicion, made to jump through hoops or simply ignored (Vandrick, 2015). This attitude sometimes extends to immigrants who have been in the US or Canada for many years, or whose parents or grandparents grew up in North America, and yet are still asked 'Where are you from?' When this question is answered with

'Chicago' or 'Colorado', the person is often asked again, 'Yes, but where are you *really* from?'

Note that these issues of 'othering' immigrants and international students are further complexified by issues of social class; as with the hierarchies experienced in missionary contexts, there are hierarchies of social class that interact with other types of 'othering'. For example, students who have social class privilege are often less affected (although still affected) by racism and xenophobia than less socially privileged students (Ramanathan & Morgan, 2009; Vandrick, 1995, 2011b).

Monolingualism in the US and the Increasing Dominance of English Elsewhere

In Chapter 6, I note that most of the MK memoirists in my study either did not learn local languages and/or did not consider it important to do so, although some in fact did learn those languages, at least to a point. I contrast this attitude and these decisions with those of immigrants and international students in North America who have little or no choice about learning English; they need to be able to use English in order to get schooling and jobs, and in general to be successful in their new country. This disparity is related to power. When someone from a more powerful country (often with a colonial history) lives in a less powerful country, and in particular when they are not staying in that country as adults, they don't really need to learn local languages. As I noted in Chapter 6, they have the 'luxury' of remaining monolingual; in fact, a large majority of North Americans (about 80%), especially those in the US (Canadian students generally learn both English and French at minimum), are monolingual (Potowski, 2010). When people from a less powerful country move to a more powerful one, the situation is reversed; they are almost forced to learn the language there, in this case English.

Yet even in non-English-dominant countries, English is becoming more and more pervasive, almost a world language. It is true that there are some advantages to this, including ease of communication among residents and travelers of different countries. However, the English language has become and continues to further become more and more imperialist. Macedo (2017: 82) states that the 'superiority complex of viewing English as the international language, the language of commerce, the language of technology that everyone wants or needs to learn, is part and parcel of' imperialism. There is a very real danger of English's gaining too much power, and even driving out other languages or allowing them to die, as many languages have already died. Phillipson (1992, 2009) has called this 'linguistic imperialism', and Skutnabb-Kangas (2000) uses the term 'linguistic genocide'. Over the past three decades there have developed academic disciplines titled World Englishes (Kachru, 1993) about varieties of English around the world, such as Singaporean English; English as an International Language, with many publications and conference papers addressing this concept of the accelerating and sometimes problematic spread of English (e.g. Holliday, 2005; Matsuda, 2017; Pennycook, 2017); and English as a Lingua Franca (publications include Jenkins, 2009; Seidlhofer, 2013). Kubota (2015) and Pennycook (2017), among others, focus on the inequalities among the ways that the various varieties of English are regarded and valued. The crux of the matter is, as always, power.

Some recent examples of scholarship pointing out the connections between colonialism and linguistic imperialism in English language teaching include publications by Hsu (2017), Johnston (2017) and Motha (2014). Regarding English language education, Hsu points out that the 'extensive colonial histories of English instruction have become a critical concern among those involved in various aspects of English language teaching, and they are especially relevant within the field of TESOL [Teaching English to Speakers of Other Languages]' (Hsu, 2017: 112). We see increasing scholarship and activism in the discipline of TESOL in response to this concern.

Motha (2014: xxi) powerfully voices her concerns regarding the colonial spread of English as follows:

> It reinforces colonial divisions of power and racial inequalities. As English is increasingly commodified, racialized, and globalized, it is implicated in the persistence of racial inequalities, in cultural and economic domination, in heritage language loss, in the extinction of less-commonly-spoken languages and their inherent epistemologies, and in inequitable distribution of global wealth and resources.

A related issue in the field of English language teaching is the way that many institutions and employers prefer 'native' speakers of English (in this case known as Native English Speaking Teachers or NESTs) to teach the language, in many cases regardless of whether they are properly educated to do so. In the meanwhile, well-educated and prepared 'non-native' speakers of English (who have learned English as an additional language) are sometimes denied jobs teaching English. Holliday (2005) has termed this bias 'native-speakerism'. Often these latter teachers (labeled 'Non-native English Speaking Teachers' or NNESTs), when they have earned teacher education degrees, are better at teaching than 'native speakers'.

Among many reasons for this is the fact that they have usually studied and learned the structure of English (including grammar) more intentionally and systematically than 'native speakers' do. In addition, they are personally familiar with the process of learning an additional language, and therefore can often understand and aid their students better. The main point, however, is that teachers of English should be judged on their individual qualifications, not as representatives of certain countries, races or varieties of English. To do otherwise is to perpetuate not only the idea that English is the dominant and most useful language in today's world, but also that only 'native speakers' of English, and only certain varieties of English (British, American, Australian) count as 'real' or 'acceptable' English. NNESTs have experienced, and still experience, discrimination in the world of English teaching, and the results have been unjust and harmful to the teachers (Braine, 1999), to students and to the field of ELT. Meanwhile, 'native' speakers of English can, like the missionary kids, blithely coast on knowing the language of domination, and can choose not to learn other languages, as the other languages are merely options, not necessary to them. Closely related is the discrimination experienced by English language teachers of color, another injustice that harms teachers and students, and taints the field of English language education (Curtis & Romney, 2006).

English Teachers as (Sometimes Covert) Missionaries

A controversial issue regarding connections between missionary work and Teaching English as a Foreign Language is that of North American missionaries or quasi-missionaries going to various countries ostensibly to teach English but meanwhile, often covertly, also doing evangelical missionary work. Sometimes this involves obtaining visas under false pretenses to countries that give visas to English teachers but do not give visas to those who are openly planning to do missionary work.

Many scholars in the field of ELT find this a huge and disturbing problem. Pennycook and Makoni (2005: 139) state that '[t]he use of English language teaching as a means to convert the unsuspecting English language learner raises profound moral and political questions about what is going on in English classrooms around the world'. They add, vividly, that '[w]ith the massive increase in the global demand for English, the language has now become the bait for the missionary hook' (p. 141).

The main issue here is this overt and covert use of ELT for religious purposes. Further, of particular concern is the deception involved in many cases. In some countries, such as China, it is against the law for foreigners to evangelize (Snow, 2001: 2), so evangelizers need to employ a certain amount of deception. In addition, often these missionaries using EFL teaching as a pretext for entering a country are neither credentialed nor well-prepared teachers. To be fair, many of the evangelical English teachers in this situation are well-prepared teachers, as well as people of integrity, and they find their own ways of justifying their positions and balancing their religion and their teaching. As with so many situations in life, there is not always a bright, clear line between right and wrong in these cases. Dormer (2011), for example, writes of her concerns about the words 'mission' and 'missionary' having taken on negative connotations. She writes of her own struggles with the idea that some people feel that being a missionary and being a professional English teacher mean different things. She decides that the most important points for Christian missionary English teachers are effectiveness and integrity, and that '*integrity* is the only way forward in meshing these two worlds' (Dormer, 2011: xvii). She further states that '[m]y English teaching is enhanced because I minister the love of Jesus Christ. My ministry is enhanced because I teach English' (p. xvii). Dormer's book includes many suggestions about how to blend these two aspects in her teaching. For example, she lists such suggestions as '[p]ray for your students'; tell your students you are Christian; 'use religious topics in class'; and '[o]ffer Christian activities outside of class (e.g., a Bible study, discipleship' (Dormer, 2011: 60). Although Dormer's intentions are good, some may feel that these activities do not ameliorate the deception involved.

Despite the Christian missionary teachers, such as Dormer, who are very aware of the issues and who do their best to reconcile their two identities (but with whose suggestions some might still disagree), it is still a problem that many teachers enter a country under false pretenses, and/or are not well-trained teachers. The consequences are that many schools and students are in effect being taken advantage of. These situations are also detrimental to the field of ELT, as they increase suspicion about the real motives of teachers and taint the reputation of the discipline itself.

Since the early 2000s, these issues have been raised and discussed by several scholars (e.g. Edge, 2003, 2006; Johnston, 2017; Johnston & Varghese, 2006; Vandrick, 2009a; Varghese & Johnston, 2007). For the title of their article on this topic, Pennycook and Coutand-Marin (2003) coined the catchy and useful phrase 'Teaching English as a Missionary Language'. Some Christian ELT educators and scholars have defended doing missionary work as part of EFL teaching (e.g. Baurain, 2007; Snow, 2001), sometimes comparing it with any other type of belief, such as social and political beliefs, that teachers have and may bring up during their classes. Other Christian ELT scholars (e.g. Purgason, 2016; Wong, 2009) have been more guarded, emphasizing the importance not only of not proselytizing, especially one's own EFL students, but also of not even appearing to proselytize. Several widely diverging perspectives on these questions about Christian English language teaching, covert or otherwise, are collected and in conversation with each other in Wong and Canagarajah (2009).

Implications for Other Western Entities

This research in this book has social justice-related implications not only for missionaries, but also for other Western (especially, but not only, North American) missionary-like projects such as those of national and international government organizations, non-governmental organizations and international charities, for their employees and their children, and for the complex, often vexed relationships among the senders/bringers of such aid and those who receive it. These issues include many that have been discussed in this book, including in this chapter.

The connections among colonialism, missionary work, ELT and related international work are complex, and there are no definitive answers for English language educators and others who do colonial-implicated, missionary-like work. I hope that this study of the MK memoirs will contribute to the discussion.

A Personal Epilogue

One day toward the end of my time writing this book, I happened to glance at a bookshelf in my home, and felt two books calling out to me. I picked up these two heavy, worn-looking books: my late father's Telugu grammar book and his Telugu dictionary. His signature is written on the inside covers in his distinctive handwriting. In the dictionary he also noted the date he acquired the book: October 27, 1952, the year my parents went to India as missionaries and immediately started studying the Telugu language. Holding my beloved father's aging but well-made hardback Telugu books in my hands, I felt their weight, gently riffled through the pages and absorbed the power of the Telugu script, so familiar and yet unreadable to me. I felt a wave of emotion as I remembered my father's love, his caring, his earnestness about learning Telugu and other Indian languages, but much more, his dedication to making a difference through his missionary work. He, like my mother, was always so supportive of my academic career and my endeavors, and read all my publications when he was alive. I know he would have been interested in and supportive of this book as well; even if he did not agree with all my assertions, he would carefully consider them. It happened that I had not looked at the Telugu books for a few years, and that the day I looked at them, I was feeling a little discouraged about all the work left to do before my own book, this one, would be finished. However, seeing and holding his books in my hand, with all their history and associations with my parents, with my own experiences, and with the topic of this book, I felt renewed energy and inspiration, almost as if my father were reassuring me and encouraging me to continue and finish writing the book. Indeed, I was able to go back to the work with renewed energy and purpose.

Throughout the process of researching and writing this book, I have experienced a rush of memories, and a mixture of emotions. Although the MK memoirists write about their times in various countries, at various time periods, at various ages, under various missions, it was surprising to me how so many of the memoirists' 'missionary kid' experiences have been similar to mine, in large ways and small. A few of the small ways are evoked by the following words and phrases found in the memoirs and sparking my own childhood memories: living on a compound, verandahs, sleeping porches, unreliable electricity, long church services in languages one doesn't understand, packages from 'home', hill stations, *chits*, tea, flannel boards, malaria, beggars, prayers before trips, long train trips to and from boarding school, separation from families, writing letters to parents every Sunday from boarding school, Jeeps, fording streams, bumpy *ghats*, using lanterns and flashlights to walk at night, the cries of hyenas and jackals at night, furloughs, voyages by ship across the Atlantic and Pacific Oceans, snakes, scorpions, tin roofs, frequent moves.

Writing this book has been for me a process that has been both an engaging, satisfying scholarly investigation and an emotional experience as I relive my own experiences as a 'missionary kid'. I have written earlier in the book about my positionality in this research, and how I believe that my own experiences both influence and enrich my understanding of the 'missionary kid' memoirs. While writing the book, I have also drawn on my love of literature, including memoirs, and on my academic and personal interest in identities, including those related to gender, race and social class. In addition, I have written that I believe that this type of research and writing, one that blends traditional academic research and the researcher's own experiences and feelings, is not only valid but also valuable, and I have tried to exemplify that practice in this book.

Here in this personal epilogue, however, I confess that, although I can honestly say that researching and writing this book has been one of the best experiences I have had in my academic life, it has also been hard at times. The biggest conflict has been between, on the one hand, my respect and love for my parents and for other missionaries who genuinely cared about helping people and made a real difference in the world and, on the other hand, my academic perspectives shaped by critical theory and postcolonial theory, leading me to critique missionary work as embodying colonialism. Also relevant is the fact that I have not identified as Christian since my adolescent years. I don't support the missionary enterprise as a whole, and see it as part of the colonial enterprise. Both too often use their positions of power to impose, or attempt to impose, their beliefs, cultures and religion on less powerful people in less powerful countries. Yet I do believe that much good has been done by missionaries; I not only saw firsthand the work my parents and their colleagues did in medicine and education, but have since seen the arguments of scholars who acknowledge and provide evidence for the good that was often done by some missions and missionaries. Nevertheless, I still live with the contradiction

References

Achebe, C. (1958) *Things Fall Apart*. London: William Heinemann.
Addleton, J.S. (1997) *Some Far and Distant Place*. Athens, GA: University of Georgia Press.
Addleton, J.S. (2000) Missionary kid memoirs: A review essay. *International Bulletin of Missionary Research* 24 (1), 30–34.
Allen, C. (1975) *Plain Tales from the Raj: Images of British India in the Twentieth Century*. London: Abacus.
Allman, J. (1994) Making mothers: Missionaries, medical officers and women's work in colonial Asante, 1924–1945. *History Workshop* 38, 23–47.
Alter, S. (1998) *All the Way to Heaven: An American Boyhood in the Himalayas*. New York: Penguin.
Austin, C.N. (1983) *Cross-cultural Reentry: An Annotated Bibliography*. Abilene, TX: Abilene Christian University.
Austin, C.N. (1986) *Cross-cultural Reentry: A Book of Readings*. Abilene, TX: Abilene Christian University.
Baller, F.W. (1907) *Letters from an Old Missionary to His Nephew*. Shanghai: American Presbyterian Mission Press.
Barkhuizen, G. (2013) Introduction: Narrative research in applied linguistics. In G. Barkhuizen (ed.) *Narrative Research in Applied Linguistics* (pp. 1–16). Cambridge: Cambridge University Press.
Bascom, T. (2006) *Chameleon Days: An American Boyhood in Ethiopia*. Boston, MA: Houghton Mifflin.
Baurain, B. (2007) Christian witness and respect for persons. *Journal of Language, Identity, and Education* 6 (3), 201–219.
Bell, J.S. (2002) Narrative inquiry: More than just telling stories. *TESOL Quarterly* 36 (2), 207–213.
Bell, L. (1996) *Hidden Immigrants: Legacies of Growing up Abroad*. Notre Dame, IN: Cross Cultural Publications.
Bellenoit, H.J.A. (2007) *Missionary Education and Empire in Late Colonial India, 1860–1920*. London: Pickering & Chatto.
Bhabha, H. (1994) *The Location of Culture*. London: Routledge.
Bhakiaraj, P.J. (2016) The church and mission in the New Testament. In B. Ekstrom (ed.) *The Church in Mission: Foundations and Global Case Studies* (pp. 51–58). Pasadena, CA: William Carey Library.
Bonk, J.J. (2007) *Missions and Money: Affluence as a Missionary Problem – Revisited* (2nd edn). Maryknoll, NY: Orbis Books.
Bowie, F. (1993) Introduction: Reclaiming women's presence. In F. Bowie, D. Kirkwood and S. Ardener (eds) *Women and Missions: Past and present: Anthropological and Historical Perceptions* (pp. 1–19). Providence, RI: Berg.

Bowie, F., Kirkwood, D. and Ardener, S. (eds) (1993) *Women and Missions: Past and Present: Anthropological and Historical Perceptions*. Providence, RI: Berg.
Braaten, C.E. (2010) *Because of Christ: Memoirs of a Lutheran Theologian*. Grand Rapids, MI: William B. Eerdmans.
Braine, G. (ed.) (1999) *Non-native Educators in English Language Teaching*. Mahwah, NJ: Lawrence Erlbaum.
Brendon, V. (2005) *Children of the Raj*. London: Phoenix.
Brownfoot, J.N. (1990) Sisters under the skin: Imperialism and the emancipation of women in Malaya, c. 1891–1941. In J.A. Mangan (ed.) *Making Imperial Mentalities: Socialisation and British Imperialism* (pp. 46–73). Manchester: University of Manchester Press.
Brush, S.E. (1998) *Farewell the Winterline: Memories of a Boyhood in India*. Bridgeport, CT: Author.
Buck, P. (1931) *The Good Earth*. New York: John Day.
Buettner, E. (2004) *Empire Families: Britons and Late Imperial India*. Oxford: Oxford University Press.
Burdell, P. and Swadener, B.B. (1999) Critical personal narrative and autoethnography: Reflections on a genre. *Educational Researcher* 28 (6), 21–26.
Burke, P.J. and Stets, J.E. (2009) *Identity Theory*. New York: Oxford University Press.
Burton, D. (1993) *The Raj at Table: A Culinary History of the British in India*. London: Faber and Faber.
Canagarajah, A.S. (2012) Teacher development in a global profession: An autoethnography. *TESOL Quarterly* 46 (2), 258–279.
Casanave, C.P. and Vandrick, S. (2003) Introduction: Issues in writing for publication. In C.P. Casanave and S. Vandrick (eds) *Writing for Scholarly Publication: Behind the Scenes in Language Education* (pp. 1–13). Mahwah, NJ: Lawrence Erlbaum.
Castro, E. (1978) Liberation, development and evangelism: Must we choose in mission? *Occasional Bulletin for Missionary Research* 2 (3), 87–91.
Cleall, E. (2012) *Missionary Discourse of Difference: Negotiating Otherness in the British Empire, 1840–1900*. London: Palgrave Macmillan.
Coleman, D. (2003) *The Scent of Eucalyptus: A Missionary Childhood in Ethiopia*. Fredericton, Canada: Goose Lane.
Collier, A.M. (2008) *Missionary Kids' Repatriation Narratives*. PhD thesis, Texas Women's University, Denton, TX.
Connelly, F.M. and Clandinin, D.J. (1999) Knowledge, context, and identity. In F.M. Connelly and D.J. Clandinin (eds) *Shaping a Professional Identity: Stories of Educational Practice* (pp. 1–5). New York: Teachers College Press.
Conrad, J. (1899) *Heart of Darkness*. London: Blackwood's.
Cordell, R. (as told to H. Knoll, Jr and H. Byler, Jr) (2008) *A Missionary's Daughter in India: The Autobiography of Ruth Cordell*. Bloomington, IN: AuthorHOUSE.
Cox, J. (2002) *Imperial Fault Lines: Christianity and Colonial Power in India, 1818–1940*. Stanford, CA: Stanford University Press.
Crenshaw, K. (1991) Mapping the margins: Intersectionality, identity politics, and violence against women of color. *Stanford Law Review* 43 (6), 1241–1299.
Curtis, A. and Romney, M. (eds) (2006) *Color, Race, and English Language Teaching: Shades of Meaning*. Mahwah, NJ: Lawrence Erlbaum.
Czarniawska, B. (2004) *Narratives in Social Science Research*. Thousand Oaks, CA: Sage.
Daiute, C. and Lightfoot, C. (eds) (2004) *Narrative Analysis: Studying the Development of Individuals in Society*. Thousand Oaks, CA: Sage.

Dangarembga, T. (2004) *Nervous Conditions*. Oxfordshire: Ayebia Clarke (original work published 1988).
Danielson, E.E. (1984) *Missionary Kid – MK*. Pasadena, CA: William Carey Library.
Dawson, M. (2009) *Growing up Yanomamo: Missionary Adventures in the American Rainforest*. Larkspur, CO: Grace Acres Press.
De Courcy, A. (2014) *The Fishing Fleet: Husband-hunting in the Raj*. New York: Harper Perennial.
Denton, J. (2003) *Foreign Devil Boy or Older Brother?: A Missionary Kid's Experiences of Life in the Orient*. Springfield, MO: Author.
Deters, G. (2009) *Divine Betrayal: An Inspirational Story of Love, Rebellion and Redemption*. Incline Village, NV: Grand Sierra.
Dilley, A.P. (2012) *Faith and Other Flat Tires: Searching for God on the Rough Road of Doubt*. Grand Rapids, MI: Zondervan.
Dinesen, I. (1937) *Out of Africa*. New York: Putnam.
Dopirak, M.H.E. (2016) *Missionary Kid: Born in India, Bound for America*. Author.
Dormer, J.E. (2011) *Teaching English in Missions*. Pasadena, CA: William Carey Library.
Dow, P. (2003) *'School in the Clouds': The Rift Valley Academy Story*. Pasadena, CA: William Carey Library.
Edge, J. (2003) Imperial troopers and servants of the lord: A vision of TESOL for the 21st century. *TESOL Quarterly* 37 (4), 701–709.
Edge, J. (ed.) (2006) *(Re)locating TESOL in an Age of Empire*. Basingstoke: Palgrave Macmillan.
Ellis, C. (2004) *The Ethnographic I: A Methodological Novel about Autoethnography*. Lanham, MD: AltaMira Press.
Espey, J. (1994) *Minor Heresies, Major Departures: A China Mission Boyhood*, Berkeley, CA: University of California Press.
Flemming, L.A. (1989) Introduction: Studying women missionaries in Asia. In L.A. Flemming (ed.) *Women's Work for Women: Missionaries and Social Change in Asia* (pp. 1–10). Boulder, CO: Westview Press.
Forster, E.M. (1952) *A Passage to India*. New York: Harcourt, Brace (original work published 1924).
Foss, M. (2001) *Out of India: A Raj Childhood*. London: Michael O'Mara.
Frerichs, C.E. (2010) *Desires of the Heart: A Daughter Remembers her Missionary Parents*. Nashville, TN: Cold River Studio.
Friesen, P R. (2003) *Ultimate Sacrifice: An Intimate Look into Missionary Boarding Schools and the Ultimate Sacrifice of the Children*. New York: iUniverse.
Frykenberg, R.E. (2003a) Christians in India: An historical overview of their complex origins. In R.E. Frykenberg (ed.) *Christians and Missionaries in India: Cross-cultural Communication Since 1500* (pp. 33–61). Grand Rapids, MI: William B. Eerdmans.
Frykenberg, R.E. (2003b) Introduction: Dealing with contested definitions and controversial perspectives. In R.E. Frykenberg (ed.) *Christians and Missionaries in India: Cross-cultural Communication Since 1500* (pp. 1–32). Grand Rapids, MI: William B. Eerdmans.
Ghosh, A. (2008) *Sea of poppies*. London: John Murray.
Gillies, W. (1998) Third culture kids: Children on the move. *Childhood Education* 75 (1), 36–38.
Goodson, I. and Gill, S. (2011) *Narrative Pedagogy: Life History and Learning*. New York: Peter Lang.

Gray, C.J. (1995) *Children of the Call: Issues Missionaries' Kids Face*. Birmingham, AL: New Hope.
Gray, L. (2014) *Three Ring Circus: Life as a Missionary Kid in a Family of 11*. Bloomington, IN: Westbow Press.
Gregory, C. (2002) Third culture kids: Returning home. *Education Today* 52 (2), 11–22.
Grimshaw, T. and Sears, C. (2008) 'Where am I from?' 'Where do I belong?': The negotiation and maintenance of identity by international school students. *Journal of Research in International Education* 7 (3), 259–278.
Haggis, J. (2000) Ironies of emancipation: Changing configurations of 'women's work' in the 'mission of sisterhood' to Indian women. *Feminist Review* 65 (summer), 108–126.
Hale, T.H. III. (2016) *Authentic Lives: Overcoming the Problem of Hidden Identity in Outreach to Restrictive Nations*. Pasadena, CA: William Carey Library.
Hancock, A.-H. (2016) *Intersectionality: An Intellectual History*. New York: Oxford University Press.
Harrison, H.B. (1983) *From M.K. to R.M.* Crawford, TX: Crawford Christian Press.
Harvey, V.P. (2009) *The Missionary Myth: Through the Eyes of a Missionary Kid*. West Conshohocken, PA: Infinity.
Hayden, M. (2006) *Introduction to International Education: International Schools and their Communities*. London: Sage.
Headland, I.T. (1912) *Some By-products of Missions*. Cincinnati, OH: Jennings & Graham.
Henderson-James, N. (2009) *At Home Abroad: An American Girl in Africa*. Austin, TX: Plain View Press.
Heusinkveld, P. (2017) *Elephant Baseball: A Missionary Kid's Tale*. Grand Rapids, MI: William B. Eerdmans.
Hill Collins, P. and Bilge, S. (2016) *Intersectionality*. Cambridge: Polity Press.
Hocking, W.E. and the Committee of Appraisal (1932) *Re-thinking Missions: A Laymen's Inquiry after One Hundred Years*. New York: Harper and Brothers.
Holliday, A. (2005) *The Struggle to Teach English as an International Language*. Oxford: Oxford University Press.
Hollinger, D.A. (2017) *Protestants Abroad: How Missionaries Tried to Change the World but Changed America*. Princeton, NJ: Princeton University Press.
Hsu, F. (2017) Resisting the coloniality of English: A research review of strategies. *CATESOL Journal* 29 (1), 111–132.
Huber, M.T. and Lutkehaus, N.C. (1999) Introduction: Gendered missions at home and abroad. In M.T. Huber and N.C. Lutkehaus (eds) *Gendered Missions: Women and Men in Missionary Discourse and Practice* (pp. 1–38). Ann Arbor, MI: University of Michigan Press.
Hunter, J. (1984) *The Gospel of Gentility: American Women missionaries in Turn-of-the-century China*. New Haven, CT: Yale University Press.
Hustad, M. (2014) *More than Conquerors: A Memoir of Lost Arguments*. New York: Farrar, Straus and Giroux.
Hutchison, W.R. (1987) *Errand to the World: American Protestant Thought and Foreign Missions*. Chicago, IL: University of Chicago Press.
Isch, C.S. (2015) When two cultures cross: Perceptions of educational leaders on the factors that support missionary kid's [sic] re-entry process to their home culture. PhD thesis, California State University, Sacramento, CA.

Jacoby, M.L.M. (2011) *Mish Kid to Mystic: Memoirs of a Missionary Daughter*. Duarte, CA: Author.
Jenkins, J. (2009) English as a lingua franca: Interpretation and attitudes. *World Englishes* 28 (2), 200–207.
Jhabvala, R. (1975) *Heat and Dust*. New York: Harper and Row.
Johnson, B.P. (2009) *If the Rains Don't Cleanse*. Los Angeles, CA: Havenhurst.
Johnston, A. (2003) *Missionary Writing and Empire, 1800–1860*. Cambridge: Cambridge University Press.
Johnston, B. (2017) *English Teaching and Evangelical Mission: The Case of Lighthouse School*. Bristol: Multilingual Matters.
Johnston, B. and Varghese, M.M. (2006) Neo-liberalism, evangelism, and ELT: Modernist missions and a postmodern profession. In J. Edge (ed.) *(Re)locating TESOL in an Age of Empire* (pp. 195–207). Basingstoke: Palgrave Macmillan.
Jordan, P. (1992) *Re-Entry: Making the Transition from Missions to Life at Home*. Seattle, WA: YWAM.
Kachru, B.B. (1993) *The Other Tongue: English Across Cultures* (2nd edn). Urbana, IL: University of Illinois Press.
Kachru, B.B. (1995) The alchemy of English. In B. Ashcroft, G. Griffiths and H. Tiffin (eds) *The Post-colonial Studies Reader* (pp. 291–295). New York: Routledge.
Kalu, O. (1980) *The History of Christianity in West Africa*. Harlow: Prentice Hall/Longman.
Kanno, Y. (2003) *Negotiating Bilingual and Bicultural Identities: Japanese Returnees Betwixt Two Worlds*. Mahwah, NJ: Erlbaum.
Kaye, M.M. (1978) *The Far Pavilions*. New York: Viking.
Kennedy, J.W. (1998 April) Missions: From trauma to truth: Once-abused children demand accountability. *Christianity Today*, 27 April 1998. See http://www.christianity today.com/ct/1998/april27/8t5016.html (accessed 11 July 2012).
Kent, E.F. (1999) Tamil Bible women and the Zenana missions of colonial South India. *History of Religions* 39 (2), 117–149.
King, M. (1989) Exporting femininity, not feminism: Nineteenth-century U.S. missionary women's efforts to emancipate Chinese women. In L.A. Flemming (ed.) *Women's Work for Women: Missionaries and Social Change in Asia* (pp. 117–135). Boulder, CO: Westview Press.
Kingsolver, B. (1999) *The Poisonwood Bible*. New York: Harper.
Knight, M. (2008) 'Our school is like the United Nations': An examination of how the discourse of diversity in schooling naturalizes whiteness and white privilege. In D. Gerin-Lajoie (ed.) *Educators' Discourses on Student Diversity in Canada: Context, Policy, and Practice* (pp. 81–108). Toronto: Canadian Scholars' Press.
Kopp, D.A. (2014) *Made in Africa*. Author.
Kramsch, C. (1993) *Context and Culture in Language Teaching*. Oxford: Oxford University Press.
Kubota, R. (1999) Japanese culture constructed by discourses: Implications for Applied Linguistics research and ELT. *TESOL Quarterly* 33 (1), 9–35.
Kubota, R. (2015) Inequalities of English, English speakers, and languages: A critical perspective on pluralist approaches to English. In R. Tupas (ed.) *Unequal Englishes: The Politics of English Today* (pp. 21–41). London: Palgrave Macmillan.
Kuegler, S. (2005) *Child of the Jungle: The True Story of a Girl Caught between Two Worlds*. New York: Warner Books.
Ladson-Billings, G. (1994) *The Dreamkeepers: Successful Teachers of African American Children*. San Francisco, CA: Jossey-Bass.

Langford, M. (2001) Global nomads, third culture kids and international schools. In M.C. Hayden and J.J. Thompson (eds) *International Education: Principles and Practice* (pp. 28–43). London: Kogan Page.

Lankina, T. and Getachew, L. (2012) Competitive religious entrepreneurs: Christian missionaries and female education in colonial and post-colonial India. *British Journal of Political Science* 43, 103–131.

Lichtman, M. (2006) *Qualitative Research in Education: A User's Guide*. Thousand Oaks, CA: Sage.

Littell, J.F. (1995) *A Lifetime in Every Moment*. New York: Houghton Mifflin.

Little, K.M. (2015) The influence of childhood mobility on adult attachment style in white missionary kids of North American and European nationalities. PhD thesis, Biola University.

Lloret, D.B. (2004) *mk.cam: Tales from the Life of an Urban Missionary Kid*. Baltimore, MD: PublishAmerica.

Lockerbie, D.B. (1975) *Education of Missionaries' Children: The Neglected Dimension of World Mission*. South Pasadena, CA: William Carey Library.

Looper, E.H. (2008) *Under His Wings: Memoirs of a West African Missionary Kid*. Tulsa, OK: Eagle Press.

Macedo, D. (2017) Imperialist desires in English-only language policy. *CATESOL Journal* 29 (1), 81–110.

MacMillan, M. (2007) *Women of the Raj: The Mothers, Wives, and Daughters of the British Empire in India*. New York: Random House (original work published 1988).

Makoni, S. and Makoni, B. (2009) English and education in Anglophone Africa: Historical and current realities. In M.S. Wong and S. Canagarajah (eds) *Christian and Critical English Language Educators in Dialogue: Pedagogical and Ethical Dilemmas* (pp. 106–119). New York: Routledge.

Masani, Z. (1987) *Indian Tales of the Raj*. Berkeley, CA: University of California Press.

Matsuda, A. (ed.) (2017) *Preparing Teachers to Teach English as an International Language*. Bristol: Multilingual Matters.

Maugham, A.S. (2005) Rain. In W.S. Maugham, *Rain and Other South Sea Stories* (pp. 1–34). Mineola, NY: Dover (original work published 1921).

Maybury, H.C. (2011) *For the Souls and Soils of India: From Ohio Farm Land to the Mission Fields of India*. Bloomington, IN: Xlibris.

Maynes, M.J., Pierce, J.L. and Laslett, B. (2008) *Telling stories: The Use of Personal Narratives in the Social Sciences and History*. Ithaca, NY: Cornell University Press.

McCaig, N. (1992) Birth of a notion. *Global Nomad Quarterly* 1 (1), 1–2.

McCaig, N. (2002) Raised in the margin of the mosaic: Global nomads balance worlds within. *International Educator* spring, 11–17.

McKay, A. (2007) Towards a history of medical missions. Review of Hardiman, D. (ed.) *Healing Bodies, Saving Souls: Medical Missions in Asia and Africa*. Amsterdam and New York: Rodopi, 2006. *Medical History*, 51, 547–551.

McMurdie, J.M. (2009) *Land of the Morning: A Civilian Internee's Poignant Memories of Sunshine and Shadows* (2nd edn). Cameron, MO: American Home School.

Meyers, M. (1995) *Swimming in the Congo*. Minneapolis, MN: Milkweed.

Michener, J. (1959) *Hawaii*. New York: Random House.

Mignolo, W. (2011) *The Darker Side of Western Modernity: Global Futures, Decolonial Options*. Durham, NC: Duke University Press.

Mishler, E.G. (2006) Narrative and identity: The double arrow of time. In A. de Fina, D. Schiffrin and M. Bamberg (eds) *Discourse and Identity* (pp. 30–47). Cambridge: Cambridge University Press.

Mizutani, S. (2011) *The Meaning of White: Race, Class, and the 'Domiciled Community' in British India 1858–1930*. Oxford: Oxford University Press.

Moll, R. (2006, March 1) Missions incredible. *Christianity Today* 50 (3), 28.

Morahan, C., O'Brien, J., Scott, P., Subik, J. and Taylor, K. (creators) (1984) *The Jewel in the Crown*. Television series. London: Granada.

Motha, S. (2014) *Race, Empire, and English Language Teaching: Creating Responsible and Ethical Anti-Racist Practice*. New York: Teachers College Press.

Nalini, M. (2006) Gender dynamics of missionary work in India and its impact on women's education: Isabella Thoburn (1840–1901) – A case study. *Journal of International Women's Studies* 7 (4), 266–289.

Nash, R.J. (2004) *Liberating Scholarly Writing: The Power of Personal Narrative*, New York: Teachers College Press.

Nehrbass, K.R. (2016) The controversial image of the US American in missions. In R.C. Scheuermann and E.L. Smither (eds) *Controversies in Mission: Theology, People, and Practice of Mission in the 21st Century* (pp. 143–164). Pasadena, CA: William Carey Library.

Nette, J. and Hayden, M. (2007) Globally mobile children: The sense of belonging. *Educational Studies* 33 (4), 435–444.

Norton, B. (2000) *Identity and Language Learning: Gender, Ethnicity and Educational Change*. New York: Longman.

Norton, B. (2013) *Identity and Language Learning: Extending the Conversation* (2nd edn). Bristol: Multilingual Matters.

Noyes, H. (1989) *China Born: Adventures of a Maverick Bookman*. San Francisco, CA: China Books & Periodicals.

Nygaard, B. (2016) Mission and ecclesiology – Why? In B. Ekstrom (ed.) *The Church in Mission: Foundations and Global Case Studies* (pp. 111–117). Pasadena, CA: William Carey Library.

Okada, H. (2009) Somewhere 'in between': Languages and identities of three Japanese international schools. PhD thesis, Temple University.

Okon, E.E. (2014) Christian missions and colonial rule in Africa. *European Scientific Journal* 10 (17), 192–209.

O'Neill, J. (2014) *The Dog*. New York: Pantheon.

Orr, E.N. (2003) *Gods of Noonday: A White Girl's African Life*. Charlottesville, VA: University of Virginia Press.

Orwell, G. (1934) *Burmese Days*. New York: Harper & Brothers.

Palmer, C. (2002) *The Happy Room*. Wheaton, IL: Tyndale.

Pennycook, A. (1998) *English and the Discourses of Colonialism*. New York: Routledge.

Pennycook, A. (2012) *Language and Mobility: Unexpected Places*. Bristol: Multilingual Matters.

Pennycook, A. (2017) *The Cultural Politics of English as an International Language*. New York: Routledge (original work published 1994).

Pennycook, A. and Coutand-Marin, S. (2003) Teaching English as a Missionary Language (TEML). *Discourse: Studies in the Cultural Politics of Education* 24 (3), 337–353.

Pennycook, A. and Makoni, S. (2005) The modern mission: The language effects of Christianity. *Journal of Language, Identity and Education* 4 (2), 137–155.

Peters, D.B. (1996) *Through Isaac's Eyes: Crossing of Cultures, Coming of Age, and the Bond between Father and Son*. Grand Rapids, MI: Zondervan.
Phemister, M.A. (2009) *Lessons from a Broken Chopstick: A Memoir of a Peculiar Childhood*. Garland, TX: Hannibal Books.
Phillips, C.J. (1969) *Protestant America and the Pagan World: The First Half Century of the American Board of Commissioners for Foreign Missions, 1810–1860*. PhD thesis, Harvard University. Cambridge, MA: Harvard University Press (original work published 1954).
Phillipson, R. (1992) *Linguistic Imperialism*. Oxford: Oxford University Press.
Phillipson, R. (2009) *Linguistic Imperialism Continued*. Hyderabad: Orient Blackswan.
Polkinghorne, D.E. (1988) *Narrative Knowing and the Human Sciences*. Albany, NY: State University of New York Press.
Pollock, D.C. and Van Reken, R.E. (2009) *Third Culture Kids: Growing up among Worlds* (revised edn). Boston, MA: Brealey (original work published 1999).
Porter, A. (2004) *Religion versus Empire? British Protestant Missionaries and Overseas Expansion, 1700–1914*. Manchester: Manchester University Press.
Potowski, K. (2010) *Language Diversity in the USA*. Cambridge: Cambridge University Press.
Pruitt, L.J. (2005) *A Looking-glass for Ladies: American Protestant Women and the Orient in the Nineteenth Century*. Macon, GA: Mercer University Press.
Purgason, K. (2016) *Professional Guidelines for Christian Teachers: How to Be a Teacher with Convictions While Respecting Those of Your Students*. Pasadena, CA: William Carey Library.
Quijano, A. (2007) Coloniality and modernity/rationality. *Cultural Studies* 21 (2–3), 168–178.
Ramanathan, V. and Morgan, B. (2009) Global warning: West-based TESOL, Class-blindness and the challenge for critical pedagogies. In F. Sharifian (ed.) *English as an International Language: Perspectives and Pedagogical Issues* (pp. 153–168). Bristol: Multilingual Matters.
Reimer, H.S. (1975) *A Growing Plant: Reflections of an 'M.K'. (Missionary's Kid)*. Kansas City, MO: Nazarene.
Richardson, L. (1997) *Fields of Play: Constructing an Academic Life*. New Brunswick, NJ: Rutgers University Press.
Robert, D.L. (1996) *American Women in Mission: A Social History of Their Thought and Practice*. Macon, GA: Mercer University Press.
Robert, D.L. (2014) Forty years of North American Missiology: A brief review. *International Bulletin of Missionary Research* 38 (1), 3–8.
Rodney, W. (1972) *How Europe Underdeveloped Africa*. London: L'Ouverture.
Rutman, P. (creator; producer) and McCulloch, D. (producer) (2015) *Indian Summers*. Television series. London: New Pictures/PBS/Biscuit Films.
Said, E.W. (1978) *Orientalism*. New York: Pantheon.
Said, E.W. (1995) Orientalism. In B. Ashcroft, G. Griffiths and H. Tiffin (eds) *The Postcolonial Studies Reader* (pp. 87–91). New York: Routledge.
Sandhu, P. (2014) The interactional and narrative construction of normative and resistant discourses about Hindi and English. *Applied Linguistics* 35 (1), 29–47.
Sanneh, L. (1990) *Translating the Message: The Missionary Impact on Culture*. Maryknoll, NY: Orbis Books.
Schmitthenner, S. (2004) *Ramblings with Ruth*. Bolivar, MO: Quiet Waters.
Schoonmaker, P. (2011) *Mish-kid Mosaic*. Author.

Schroeder, J.H. (2013) *Under an African Sky: The Unusual Life of a Missionaries' Kid in Ethiopia*. Agassiz, Canada: Summer Bay Press.
Schroth, G.H. (2011) *Curry, Corduroy and the Call: A Mennonite Missionary's Daughter Grows up in Rural India*. Denver, CO: Outskirts Press.
Scott, P.M. (1976) *The Raj Quartet*. New York: Morrow (original work published 1966–1974).
Scott, P.M. (1998) *Staying On*. Chicago, IL: University of Chicago Press (original work published 1977).
Seaman, P.A. (1997) *Paper Airplanes in the Himalayas: The Unfinished Path Home*. Notre Dame, IN: Cross Cultural Publications.
Seidlhofer, B. (2013) *Understanding English as a Lingua Franca*. Oxford: Oxford University Press.
Servid, C. (2000) *Of Landscape and Longing: Finding a Home at the Water's Edge*. Minneapolis, MN: Milkweed.
Sharkey, J. (2004) Lives stories don't tell: Exploring the untold in autobiographies. *Curriculum Inquiry* 34 (4), 495–512.
Sidwell, M. (2012) George Liele: Missions Pioneer. In R.J. Stevens and B. Johnson (eds) *Profiles of African-American Missionaries* (pp. 9–12). Pasadena, CA: William Carey Library.
Skarsten, M. (1992, Summer) Going home 'emotionally'. *The Enterprise: The World Mission Magazine from Canadian Baptist International Ministries* 336, 28–30.
Skutnabb-Kangas, T. (2000) *Linguistic Genocide in Education – Or Worldwide Diversity and Human Rights?* New York: Routledge.
Smith, H. (with J. Paine) (2010) *Tales of Wonder: Adventures Chasing the Divine*. New York: HarperOne.
Snow, D. (2001) *English Teaching as Christian Mission: An Applied Theology*. Scottdale, PA: Herald Press.
Spigelman, C. (2004) *Personally Speaking: Experience as Evidence in Academic Discourse*. Carbondale, IL: Southern Illinois University Press.
Stevens, R.J. (2012a) AFA rise in mission: 1976–present. In R.J. Stevens and B. Johnson (eds) *Profiles of African-American missionaries* (pp. 229–230). Pasadena, CA: William Carey Library.
Stevens, R.J. (2012b) African American outreach begins: 1700s–1780s. In R.J. Stevens and B. Johnson (eds) *Profiles of African-American missionaries* (pp. 7–8). Pasadena, CA: William Carey Library.
Stoler, A.L. (1991) Carnal knowledge and imperial power: Gender, race and morality in colonial Asia. In M. di Leonardo (ed.) *Gender at the Crossroads of Knowledge: Feminist Anthropology in the Postmodern Era* (pp. 51–101). Berkeley, CA: University of California Press.
Terry, R.J. (2011) *Help Me be a Good Girl Amen: My Journey from Missionary Kid to Truth*. Custer, WA: Brandy Wine Press.
The Editors of Time-Life Books (1999) *What Life Was Like in the Jewel in the Crown: British India AD 1600–1905*. Alexandria, VA: Time-Life Books.
Thorne, S. (1999) Missionary-imperial feminism. In M.T. Huber and N.C. Lutkehaus (eds) *Gendered Missions: Women and Men in Missionary Discourse and Practice* (pp. 39–65). Ann Arbor, MI: University of Michigan Press.
Tompkins, J. (1996) *A Life in School: What the Teacher Learned*. Berkeley, CA: Perseus Press.
Useem, R.H. (1966) The American family in India. *Annals of the American Academy of Political and Social Science*, 368, 132–145.

Useem, R.H. (1976) Third culture kids. *Today's Education* 65 (3), 103–105.
Vallgårda, K. (2015) *Imperial Childhoods and Christian Mission: Education and Emotions in South India and Denmark*. Basingstoke: Palgrave Macmillan.
Vallgårda, K. (2016) Were Christian missionaries colonizers? *Interventions: International Journal of Postcolonial Studies* 18 (6), 865–886.
Vandrick, S. (1995) Privileged ESL University Students. *TESOL Quarterly* 29 (2), 375–381.
Vandrick, S. (1999a) ESL and the colonial legacy: A teacher faces her 'missionary kid' past. In G. Haroian-Guerin (ed.) *The Personal Narrative: Writing Ourselves as Teachers and Scholars* (pp. 63–74). Portland, ME: Calendar Islands.
Vandrick, S. (1999b, July/August) Passages from India. *American Language Review* 3 (4), 27–29.
Vandrick, S. (2009a) A former 'missionary kid' responds. In M.S. Wong and S. Canagarajah (eds) *Christian Educators and Critical Practitioners in Dialogue: Ethical Dilemmas in English Language Teaching* (pp. 141–149). New York: Routledge.
Vandrick, S. (2009b) *Interrogating Privilege: Reflections of a Second Language Educator*. Ann Arbor, MI: University of Michigan Press.
Vandrick, S. (2011a, June) Comparing identities of immigrant and international students vs. 'third culture kids'. Paper presented at the meeting of the International Society for Language Studies, Aruba.
Vandrick, S. (2011b) Students of the new global elite. *TESOL Quarterly* 45 (1), 160–169.
Vandrick, S. (2013) 'The colonial legacy' and 'missionary kid' memoirs. In G. Barkhuizen (ed.) *Narrative Research in Applied Linguistics* (pp. 19–40). Cambridge: Cambridge University Press.
Vandrick, S. (2015) No 'knapsack of invisible privilege' for ESL university students. *Journal of Language, Identity, and Education* 14 (1), 54–59.
Vandrick, S. (2017, March) Colonial discourses of 'the exotic' in missionary settings and in ESL 'foods and festivals' approaches. Paper presented at the meeting of the American Association for Applied Linguistics, Portland, OR.
Vandrick, S. (2018) Multiple, complex and fluid religious and spiritual influences on English language educators. In M.S. Wong and A. Mahboob (eds) *Spirituality and English Language Teaching: Religious Explorations of Teacher Identity, Pedagogy and Context* (pp. 103–118). Bristol: Multilingual Matters.
Van Reken, R.E. (1988) *Letters Never Sent*. Indianapolis, IN: 'Letters'.
Van Valkenburg, C.T. (2014) *37 Blessings of Growing up as a Missionary Kid: The Lord Saves Those Crushed in Spirit*. Author.
Varghese, M. and Johnston, B. (2007) Evangelical Christians and English language teaching. *TESOL Quarterly* 41 (1), 5–31.
Viser, W.C. (1986) *It's OK to be an MK: What It's Like to be a Missionary Kid*. Nashville, TN: Broadman Press.
Viswanathan, G. (1995) The beginnings of English literary study in British India. In B. Ashcroft, G. Griffiths and H. Tiffin (eds) *The Post-colonial Studies Reader* (pp. 431–437). New York: Routledge.
Walls, W.J. (2012) AME and AMEZ history. In R.J. Stevens and B. Johnson (eds) *Profiles of African-American Missionaries* (pp. 22–31). Pasadena, CA: William Carey Library.
Walters, D. (2007) *The Untold Story: Missionary Kids Speak from the Ends of the Earth*. Chapel Hill, NC: Chapel Hill Press.

Welch, I. (2005) Women's work for women: Women missionaries in 19th century China. Paper presented at the eighth Women in Asia Conference, September 20–28, 2005, Sydney.

Wiebe, V.B. (with Wiebe, M.D.) (1990) *Sepia Prints: Memoirs of a Missionary in India*. Winnipeg: Kindred Press.

Willard-Traub, M.K. (2006) Reflection in academe: Scholarly writing and the shifting subject. *College English* 68 (4), 422–432.

Witherell, C. and Noddings, N. (1991) *Stories Lives Tell: Narrative and Dialogue in Education*. New York: Teachers College Press.

Wong, M.S. (2009) Deconstructing/reconstructing the missionary English teacher identity. In M.S. Wong and S. Canagarajah (eds) *Christian and Critical English Language Educators in Dialogue: Pedagogical and Ethical Dilemmas* (pp. 91–105). New York: Routledge.

Wong, M.S. and Canagarajah, S. (eds) (2009) *Christian and Critical English Language Educators in Dialogue: Pedagogical and Ethical Dilemmas*. New York: Routledge.

Woodberry, R. (2012) The missionary roots of liberal democracy. *American Political Science Review* 106 (2), 244–274.

Zinsser, W. (1998) *Inventing the Truth: The Art and Craft of Memoir*. New York: Mariner Books.

Zylstra, S.E. (2010) Boarding bust: Schools for missionary kids see lower attendance: Recent reports of child abuse overshadow another trend, *Christianity Today*, 27 December 2010. See www.christianitytoday.com/ct/2011/january/3.12.html (accessed 11 July 2016).

Zylstra, S.E. (2014) When abuse comes to light: How a generation of children, sexually abused overseas, aims to protect others before it happens. *Christianity Today*, 20 February 2014. See www.christianitytoday.com/ct/2014/march/sexual-abuse-comes-to-light.html (accessed 31 July 2015).

Index

abandonment, feelings of 9, 70–72, 77–78
abuse 69, 73–75
Achebe, China 53
Addleton, J. S. 31, 33, 34, 43, 46, 49–50, 61, 68, 71–72, 89, 98
'adventures' 42, 43, 96
affordances xiii
Africa *see also specific countries*
 animals 44–45
 ayahs/amahs/nannies 58–59
 colonialism xi, 27, 53
 exoticization of local people 47
 gender roles 98
 landscape 48
 local authors 53
 non-Western scholarship 24–25
 and race 100, 101
African-American missionaries 100
age of memoirists 32
alcoholism 22
alienation 9
Allen, C. 121
Alter, S. 1, 2, 27, 33, 34, 47, 62, 66, 75, 76, 78, 83, 87, 105, 107
Angola 62, 84, 86, 104
animals 44–45, 97, 111
Applied Linguistics 17, 113
autobiography 27, 28–29
autoethnography 28, 29, 30
ayahs/amahs/nannies 57–59, 82, 84

Baller, F.W. 56
Barkhuizen, G. 37
Bascom, T. 10, 33, 34, 47, 48, 70, 71, 76
Bell, J.S. 29
Bellenoit, H.J.A. 16, 23

belonging, sense of 7, 9, 22
Bhabha, H. 7, 39
Bhakiaraj, P.J. 11, 13
Bingham Academy, Ethiopia 33
boarding schools 9, 22, 59, 62, 64, 65, 66, 68–75, 77, 78
Bonk, J.J. 106–107
Bowie, F. 89, 90, 105
Braaten, C.E. 28, 33, 34, 77
Braine, G. 116
Brazil 83
Brendon, V. 64, 66
British missionaries 13, 23, 25, 52
British Raj in India 2, 27, 42, 52, 65, 99, 107, 121
Brush, S.E. 34, 66
Bryant, Kobe 8
bubble, living in a 59
Buck, Pearl 5, 8
Buettner, E. 42, 65, 107
Burdell, P. 28
Burton, D. 121

Cameroun 45
Canadian missionary project 12, 17, 25
Canagarajah, Suresh xi, 29, 118
career missionaries versus short-term volunteers 13, 15
Carey, William 12, 100
Casanave, Christine Pearson 28
caste system 58, 102
Castro, E. 12
ceremonies and rituals 47, 111
China
 allowing missionary work 14
 ayahs/amahs/nannies 58, 84

134

English Language Teaching
  116–117
  food 45
  local languages 84, 85
  and Orientalism 40, 41
  racism 101
  schools 67
  servants 53, 62
  women missionaries 94
Christianity
  and colonialism 4, 20–21, 23–24
  domestic evangelism 93
  and English Language Teaching xv,
  117–118
  history of missionary enterprise xi,
  11–13, 20
  and 'progress' 40
  schools 66
  and Western civilization 42
civil rights 22
Clandinin, D.J. 27
classism 51, 101
Cleall, E. 56
clichés 44–45 see also stereotypes
Coleman, D. 27, 33, 34, 42, 44, 60, 62,
  70, 72, 83, 97, 104, 106
colonialism
  and Christianity 4, 20–21, 23–24
  and English 80
  and gender 90, 91, 94
  and language 115
  in literature 52–53
  and missionaries xi, xii, 6, 13,
  19–27, 69
  and race 101
  scholarship on 4
  and schooling 64–65
  and sense of superiority 51
  and slavery 100
  and white power 103
coloniality 4, 103
communication technologies
  15, 71
condescension 43, 51–54, 55, 59, 103,
  105, 113
Connelly, F.M. 27
Conrad, Joseph 53

conservatism 69
conversion-oriented missions
  3, 55–56, 100
Cordell, R. 10, 34, 44, 83, 104
cosmopolitanism 22
Costa Rica 76
Coutand-Marin, S. 16, 117
Cox, J. 26, 90–91, 102
Curtis, A. 116
Czarniawska, B. xv, 38

Daiute, C. 28
Dalat School, Vietnam 33
Dangarembga, Tsitsi 53
danger 49
Danish Missionary Society 3
data sources 30–34
Davidson, B. xi
Dawson, M. 34, 43
De Courcy, A. 121
decoloniality xiii
decolonization 21, 104
dehumanization 55, 56
democracy 6
Denton, J. 34, 41, 47, 60, 85
depression 9
Deters, G. 34, 44, 48, 49, 83
DeVault, Marjorie 38
developed/developing countries 6, 13,
  41, 110
Dilley, A.P. 34, 85
Dinesen, Isak 53
domestic evangelism 93
Dopirak, M.H.E. 31
Dormer, J.E. 117
Dow, P. 67, 107
Dubai 51, 60

economic privilege 106–107
ecumenical denominations 21
Edge, J. 16
education-oriented missions 3, 6, 19,
  95, 120
Ellis, Carolyn 29
English 87–88, 110, 114–116
English as a Foreign Language (EFL)
  16, 117

English as a Lingua Franca (ELF) xv, 115
English as a Second Language (ESL) 113
English as an International Language (EIL) 115
English Language Teaching (ELT) xi, xv, 17, 113, 115–118
English-language schools 67
Espey, J. 34, 56, 67, 85
Ethiopia 27, 44, 62, 72, 76, 83, 104, 106
ethnocentrism 41
Eurocentricity xiii, 39
evangelical denominations 21, 95
evangelization xv, 3, 14, 100, 116–117
everyday, as source of authority 28
exoticization 16, 39–50, 111–113
expatriate communities 51
expertise of missionaries, valuing 21

false-bottomed friendships 54
famous 'third culture kids' 8
fatherhood 10
fear 49
feminism
  data analysis 33–34, 37
  narrative inquiry 28
  and race 102–103
  'single lady' missionaries 92
  and women missionaries 92, 94
Firth, Colin 8
Fleming, Daniel Johnson 40–41
Flemming, L.A. 92, 93, 94
food 45–46, 49, 111, 112
'Foods and Festivals' 111–112
Forster, E.M. 52
Foss, M. 65
fostering 68
Frerichs, P.R. 34, 46, 53–54, 60, 83
friendships 10, 62, 66, 71, 84, 97, 104
Friesen, P.R. 8, 33, 73, 74, 77
Frykenberg, R.E. 12, 20, 23
fundamentalist Christians 21, 26, 94–95
furloughs 10, 15, 48, 50, 71, 75, 76, 78, 83, 85, 107

gender
  of memoirists 33, 34
  and the missionary project 89–98
  and race 102–103
  and schooling 65
genres xii, 29
geography 48
Getachew, L. 95
Ghosh, Amitav 53
global nomads 7
Global North/Global South 6, 110
globalization 112, 115
Godden, Rumer 42
Gordimer, N. 5
grandparents, lack of relationship with 11
Gray, L. 32, 34, 47
Gregory, C. 75
Guinea 73, 74

Hale, T.H. III. 14
hardships, exoticization of 48–49
Harrison, Helen Bagby 30, 34, 48
Harvey, V.P. 8, 10, 26–27, 34, 55–56, 68, 73, 74, 77, 87
Headland, I.T. 19, 40
'heathens' 40, 56, 67, 94, 95, 101, 103
Henderson-James, N. 35, 45, 46, 62, 70, 83–84, 86, 97–98, 104, 108
Hersey, John 8
Heusinkveld, P. 31
history of missionary work 11–13, 19–27, 100
Hocking Report (1932) 3
Holliday, A. 115
Hollinger, D.A. 3, 5, 21, 22, 23, 41, 91, 100
'home,' concepts of 8, 22
'home,' returning 9–10, 22, 75–78, 86, 97, 107
'home' countries 7, 8, 9, 75–78
homeschooling 33, 66
homesickness 69, 70–72
honorary titles 101, 105
Hsu, F. 115
Huber, M.T. 90, 91, 95, 102
Hunter, J. 53, 90, 92, 93, 101
Hustad, M. 32, 35, 42, 55

Hutchison, W.R. 5, 6, 12, 41
hybrid genres xiii, xiv, 29–30, 120
hybrid identities 8, 76, 104

ignorance, 'rescue' from 42, 95, 103
illnesses 48
image, presenting a godly 10
immigration 8–9, 51, 88, 111–112
imperialism
   and English language 114–115
   and gender 90
   and missionaries 6, 20, 21, 23, 24, 25, 27
   and presumption of marginality 26
   and race 101, 102
India
   ayahs/amahs/nannies 57, 58
   British missionaries 23
   British Raj 2, 27, 42, 52, 65, 99, 107, 121
   caste system 58, 102
   Christian mission work 12, 20
   English in 86
   exoticization of local people 46
   history of missionary enterprise 12
   Kodaikanal School 22, 32, 33, 66, 107
   languages 81
   local languages 81, 82
   local people 83
   missionary schools 67
   Ootacumund school 65
   race 99
   racism 101–102, 104
   restrictions on mission work 14
   schools 64–66, 76
   social class 105
   treatment of local people 52, 63
   women missionaries 90–91, 94, 95
Indian Summers (Rutnam, 2015) 52
indigenous societies *see also* local people
   agency of 24
   missionaries' close contact with 21
Indonesia 43, 45, 46
insider-outsider status xii, 7, 37–38
international schools 66, 67, 84
international students 111–112, 113

International Voluntary Services 22
intersectionality 89, 96, 97, 99, 102–103

Jacoby, M.L.M. 35, 45, 48, 69
Jamaica 100
Japan 41, 113
Jaworski, A. xii
Johnson, B.P. 31
Johnston, A. 16, 23–24, 41, 101
Johnston, B. xiii–xiv, 54, 87–88, 98, 115
Judd, Walter 22
Judson, Adoniram and Ann 12

Kachru, B. 110, 115
Kalu, O. 25
Kanno, Y. 9
Kaye, M.M. 52
Kennedy, J.W. 74
Kent, E.F. 92
Kenya 19, 53, 67, 106
Kerry, John 8
King, M. 91, 94
Kingsolver, B. 1, 5
Kodaikanal School, India 22, 32, 33, 66, 107
Kopp, D.A. 32, 35, 42, 43–44, 45, 48, 49, 54–55, 104
Kramsch, C. 7
Kubota, R. 113, 115
Kuegler, S. 31, 32, 35, 43, 45, 46, 48, 84, 87

landscape 48
languages xv, 80–88 *see also* English; local languages
Lankina, T. 95
Laos 54, 103
lasting effects 49–50
Laubach, Frank 22
length of missionary service 15
letters (genre) 29
liberalism 21, 23, 41
Lichtman, M. 37
Liele, George 100
Lightfoot, C. 28
literary analysis 33–34
Littell, J.F. 28, 35, 45, 62, 77–78

Little, K.M. 10
Livingstone, David 12
Lloret, D.B. 8, 35, 49, 60, 68, 76, 86
local languages 80–88, 97, 101, 110, 114, 116, 119
local people
    close relationships with 54–55, 56, 57, 62, 97, 101
    condescension, criticism and mocking of 51–54
    exoticization of 46–47
    learning local languages from 84
    missionary schools 67–68
    and racism 101
    stereotypes 54–55
    superiority over 49, 51, 55–56, 58, 59
    treatment of servants 56–63
    women missionaries working with local women 93, 94, 95–96
local schools 67
Lockerbie, D.B. 59, 64
Looper, E.H. 35, 42, 44, 45, 46, 47, 57, 61, 83, 98
loss, feelings of 9
Luce, Henry 8
Lutkehaus, N.C. 90, 91, 95, 102

Macedo, D. 114
MacMillan, M. 90
Makoni, B. 81
Makoni, S. 81, 110, 116
Mamou Academy 73, 74
marginality, presumption of 26, 111, 112
Masani, Z. 121
Matheson, Arthur 15
Maugham, Somerset 5
Maybury, H.C. 35, 54, 55, 96
McCaig, N. 7
McKay, A. 20, 21
McMurdie, J.M. 35, 87
medical/education-oriented missions 3, 6, 19, 120
memoirs
    as research source 4, 17
    role of narrative in research xiii, 27–30

memory, fragility of 30
Mercury, Freddie 8
Mexico 86
Meyers, M. 31
Michener, J. 5
Middle East 14, 39
Mignolo, W. xii, xiii
Mishler, E.G. 30
missionaries
    and colonialism 20–21
    criticisms of 14, 23–24, 55
    diversity of 3–4, 21
    English Teachers as 116–118
    evolution of 13–16, 110
    gender of 89–91
    history of 11–13, 19–27
    overview 5–7
    questioning the entire enterprise 55
    scholarship on 20
    surreptitious missionary work 15, 16, 116–181
missionary schools 2, 66, 67–68, 75, 84
missology 14
Mizutani, S. 99
mnemonic traces xiv
Moll, R. 31
Morahan, C. 52
Mortensen, Viggo 8
Motha, S. 115
multiculturalism 21, 22
multigenerational effects 78
Murree Christian School, Pakistan 33, 67

Nalini, M. 93
nannies/amahs/ayahs 57–59, 82, 84
narrative inquiry xii, 27–30, 33–34, 37
Nash, R.J. 29
Native English Speaking Teachers (NESTs) 115–116
native-speakerism 115
negative connotations of missions 5–6, 23, 30
Nehrbass, K.R. 14, 80
New Guinea 46, 83
New Tribes Mission 74
Nigeria 59, 60, 67, 78, 84, 97, 104, 106, 107

Noddings, N. 28
Non-native English Speaking Teachers' (NNESTs) xv, 115–116
non-Western scholarship 24–25
novels 31, 52–53, 107, 121
Noyes, H. 35, 58, 84
Nygaard, B. 13

Obama, Barack 8
objectivity 30
Okon, E.E. 24–25, 101
O'Neill, Joseph 51, 60
one-way missions 13
Ootacumund school 65
oppression, memoirs have little evidence of awareness of 26
Orientalism 39–40, 95
orphanages 67, 68
Orr, E.N. 8, 27, 33, 35, 47, 58–59, 60, 67, 70, 72, 73, 76, 84, 86, 96–97, 103–104, 106, 107
Orwell, George 53
Othering 3, 39, 41–43, 50, 111–114
outsider status 7, 37–38, 77

'pagans' 40
Pakistan 33, 46, 50, 67, 98, 108
Palmer, C. 31, 107
parasites/worms 48
paternalism 24, 62, 101, 102
patriarchy 21, 98, 103
patronizing attitudes 3
Peace Corps 22
Pennycook, Alistair xiii–xiv, 16, 29, 40, 110, 115, 116, 117
Pentecost 11
personal academic discourse 29
Peters, D.B. 35, 70
Phemister, M.A. 8, 35, 42, 68
Philippines 47, 85, 87
Phillips, C.J. 40
Phillipson, R. 114–115
photographs 45, 122
physical abuse 73
Poisonwood Bible, The (Kingsolver, 1998) 1, 5
Pollock, D.C. 7

Porter, A. 20, 23
postcolonialism xiv, xv, 2–3, 4, 16, 19–27, 93, 120
Potowski, K. 80, 114
power disparities
  and colonialism xii, 55
  and gender 90, 94–95, 98
  and language 85, 87–88, 110, 114, 115
  narrative inquiry 37
  and race 102, 103
  and servants 57
Prawer Jhabvala, Ruth 52
'primitives' 42, 43, 46
privilege
  in colonial context 16, 69, 79
  and gender 97
  and language 80, 81, 85, 87–88
  memoirs have little evidence of awareness of 26, 60
  and race 103
  and servants 60, 61
  and social class 105–106, 114
  wealth 106–107
progressives 23, 37
proselytizing 23
Protestant denominations 3–4
Pruitt, L.J. 39, 40, 95
psychological aspects 9–11, 22, 73–74, 77–78
publishers (of memoirs) 33

qualitative research 27–28, 33–34

race 99–104, 115, 116
racism 21, 22, 47, 50, 51–52, 54–55, 65–66, 96, 101–102, 104, 114
reflective writing 28, 29
Reimer, H.S. 32, 35, 71
reintegration into North American society 9–10, 22, 75–78, 86, 97, 107
Reischauer, Edwin 21
religion
  and English Language Teaching 116–117
  and the evolution of the missionary enterprise 13, 19

religion (*Continued*)
  and missionaries 20, 68–69, 70, 73
  and re-entry into North American life 77
  representing a 10
  'rightness' of 55
  superiority (assumed) of missionaries' 56
  women as religious leaders 92
Richardson, Laurel 29
rituals 47, 111
Robert, D.L. 13, 15, 90, 94, 95
Rodney, W. 25
romanticization 30, 42, 43
Romney, M. 116
rudeness 52, 60

sahib 101, 105
Said, Edward 26, 39, 90
Sandhu, P. 81
Sanneh, L. 25
Schmitthenner, S. 35, 71
scholarly personal narrative 29
schooling
  Bingham Academy, Ethiopia 33
  boarding schools 9, 22, 59, 62, 64, 65, 66, 68–75, 77, 78
  Dalat School, Vietnam 33
  English-language schools 67
  homeschooling 33, 66
  international schools 66, 67, 84
  Kodaikanal School, India 22, 32, 33, 66, 107
  and local languages 84–85
  local schools 67
  of memoirists 33
  missionary schools 2, 66, 67–68, 75, 84
  Murree Christian School, Pakistan 33, 67
  Ootacumund school 65
  and race 104
  and separation 65, 68, 70
  and social class 65, 66
  Woodstock (missionary school, India) 2, 33, 66
Schoonmaker, P. 2, 29, 35, 42, 46, 47, 49, 66, 97

Schroeder, J.H. 36, 42, 60, 70, 72, 84, 97
Schroth, G.H. 8, 36, 44, 55, 56–57, 58, 70, 105
Scott, Paul 52, 121
scrapbooks 29
Seaman, P.A. 8, 11, 33, 36, 48, 67, 73, 108
semi-autobiographical works 31
sending/receiving nations 5, 13
Senegal 74
separation
  cycles of 10
  from parents 9, 10–11, 22, 65, 68, 70–73
  at school 65, 68, 70
  servants, treatment of 51–52, 53, 56–63
Servid, Carolyn 106, 107
sexism 96, 97, 98
sexual abuse 73
sexual identity 89
Shanghai American School 33
Sharkey, J. 28
Sheppard, William Henry 100
Sidwell, M. 100
'single lady' missionaries 91–92, 94
Skarsten, M. 70–71
Skutnabb-Kangas, T. 115
slavery 47, 54, 57, 100
Smith, Huston 30, 33, 36
snakes 44
Snow, D. 117
Sobel, Margaret 102
social class
  British Raj 99
  classism 51, 101
  coloniality 103
  and English 80, 81, 88
  and the missionary project 104–109, 114
  and privilege 69, 97
  schools 65, 66
social effects, long-term 9–11
social justice 16, 21, 118
Soper, Edmund Davidson 22
South America 43, 113
South Korea 31

Spigelman, C. 29
spiritual abuse 74
Spivak, Gayatri 39
stereotypes 39, 40, 47, 53–54, 91, 101, 103, 112
Stevens, R.J. 100
subaltern history 26
suicide 10, 22
superiority 49, 51, 55–56, 58, 59, 82, 101, 103, 113
Swadener, B.B. 28
Swaziland 71, 85

telegrams 15
Terry, R.J. 36, 42, 57, 60–61
TESOL (Teaching English to Speakers of Other Languages) xii, 115
theological differences in missions 3–4
therapy/counseling 9, 11, 74
Third Culture Kids (TCKs) 7–9, 75
Thorburn, Isabella 93
Thorne, S. 95, 102, 105
Thurlow, C. xii
Thurman, Uma 8
Tompkins, Jane 29
transitions back 'home' 9–10, 22, 75–78, 86, 97, 107
trauma 77–78
travel, exoticization of 48
travel, modern ease of 15
truth, in narratives 28
Turkey 14

'unusual,' meaning exotic 42, 44–50, 111
Upper Volta 45
Useem, R.H. 7, 16

Vallgårda, K. 3, 19–20, 24, 57–58, 67
van Lier, L. xiii
Van Reken, R.E. 7, 10–11, 29, 36, 77, 78
Van Valkenburg, C.T. 36, 42, 54, 70, 103
Vandrick, Stephanie xii, 8, 17, 28, 29, 30, 45, 106, 112, 113, 114, 121
Venezuela 43
Vietnam 33
Vietnam War 13
vignettes 29
visa rules 14, 116
Viswanathan, G. 23

Walls, W.J. 100
Walsh, C. xii, xiii
Walters, D. 9, 10, 73–74, 98
Western bias 8, 39
Wiebe, V.B. 29, 30, 36
Wilder, Thornton 8
Willard-Traub, M.K. 27, 28
Witherell, C. 28
Witherspoon, Reese 8
women
  in Africa 21
  and Christianity 21
  and missionary work 89–98, 102, 105
Women's Studies 17
Wong, M.S. xi, 118
Woodberry, R. 6
Woodstock (missionary school, India) 2, 33, 66
world citizens 23
World Englishes 115

Zambia 54
Zinsser, W. 28, 29
Zylstra, S.E. 73, 74, 75

For Product Safety Concerns and Information please contact our EU Authorised Representative:

Easy Access System Europe

Mustamäe tee 50

10621 Tallinn

Estonia

gpsr.requests@easproject.com

www.ingramcontent.com/pod-product-compliance
Ingram Content Group UK Ltd.
Pitfield, Milton Keynes, MK11 3LW, UK
UKHW021941200326
4879IPUK00004B/47